# A MEDIC'S
# MIND

# A MEDIC'S
# MIND

MATTHEW HENEGHAN

echo
BOOKS

an imprint of
Wintertickle Press

Wintertickle Press
132 Commerce Park Drive, Unit K, Ste. 155
Barrie, Ontario L4N 0Z7

*Wintertickle Press is committed to publishing works of quality and integrity.
However, the opinions, the story, the experiences, and the words in this book are
solely those of the author and not necessarily those of Wintertickle Press.*

Cover design: Heather Down
Photographs: Courtesy of Matthew Heneghan

Library and Archives Canada Cataloguing in Publication

Title: A medic's mind / Matthew Heneghan.
Names: Heneghan, Matthew, author.
Identifiers: Canadiana (print) 2019017059X | Canadiana (ebook)
20190170603 | ISBN 9781894813976 (softcover) | ISBN 9781894813990
(EPUB) | ISBN 9781989664001 (Kindle)
Subjects: LCSH: Heneghan, Matthew. | LCSH: Heneghan, Matthew—Mental
health. | LCSH: Post-traumatic stress disorder—Patients—Canada—Biography.
| LCSH: Depressed persons—Canada—Biography. | LCSH: Canada. Canadi-
an Armed Forces—Medical personnel—Biography. | LCSH: Canada—Armed
Forces—Medical personnel—Biography. | LCSH: Emergency medical techni-
cians—Canada—Biography. | LCGFT: Autobiographies.

Classification: LCC RC552.P67 H46 2019 | DDC 616.85/210092—dc23

www.wintericklepress.com
www.amedicsmind.com

*To all those I have served with and alongside,*
*and all those who serve us now*

# CONTENTS

# AUTHOR'S NOTE

THIS IS A MEMOIR. IT is a collection of my memories and perceptions. Please note this is *my* medic's mind, not a reflection of *all* medics' minds. My recollections, my experiences, and my reactions are mine personally, and not necessarily those of military personnel or paramedics as a whole. I want to share my story, my truth, and my healing.

Many names of people, dates, sequences, and details of calls have been changed to protect the privacy of others, especially my medic partners and patients.

I feel it is important to note that this is a journey toward hope. However, I would like the reader to be aware that I have experienced and been witness to a significant amount of varied trauma in my life, and at many points have felt completely hopeless. Please note that I do write about some select events within this book.

# FOREWORD

By Todd McGowan, Chief Warrant Officer (Retired),
Canadian Armed Forces

FIRST AND FOREMOST, MATT IS a man of character and integrity. Honesty, in all of its most brutal and elegant forms, is crucial to his well-being. Matt came to work for me fifteen years ago at 1 Field Ambulance in Edmonton as a happy, shiny young soldier. He was a smart, a witty, and a funny young man, always prepared to do whatever it took for his country. His selected career in medicine was proof positive of his simple desire to help people, even in the most difficult of circumstances.

The evolution of his career through the army and subsequent paramedicine field consistently took him into the most traumatic of circumstances. Within those treacherous circumstances lies the potential for deep moral injury. And as his exposures grew and grew, the inevitability of injury followed. At a certain point, the very best of humans will finally break, with long-lasting implications. Through his vast experiences and emotional pain, Matt sought to find a way to express himself and to also mindfully walk the path of recovery. His deeply emotional stories connect us intimately with the tortured psyche of a man who gave his all. I will always be proud to call Matt a friend.

# PART I

# THE FIRST JACKET

Men's, dark green, land
Size: 7338
August, 1988
Shell: 65% Wool / 35% Polyester

YOU MAY HAVE HEARD THE term "worn a lot of hats." Well, I have not owned many hats, at least not in the way the phrase is meant. Jackets, though, I have acquired and worn plenty of those. Jackets of all sizes, shapes, materials, and purposes. And the most painful thing I ever had to do was take them off.

My first jacket was not gifted to me; it was earned. And to this day, and likely for the rest of my life, it will remain one of the most important and influential garments I have ever worn. It has seen death, celebration of life, graduations, and achievements. It has hugged my skin as the rest of me rattled on those cold, unforgiving days. It is a jacket that boasts respect, devotion, and honour. It is a rare coat worn by only a few—a damn few.

Tape measures, pins, and chalk lines gave this jacket life. And when it was given to me, to hold, to wear, and to care for, it grew with me as well. First, no chevrons, then one, then two—Corporal Heneghan. That's what my jacket screamed to the world. Its immaculate buttons gleamed when embraced by the luminous sun. Badges and accoutrements adorned the tunic, proudly on display, boasting a humble pride—maybe even some bravado.

CHAPTER 1

# Valentine's Day

A HEAVY SILENCE BLANKETS THE room. She looks at me while my gaze bounces between her feet and an arbitrary patch on the floor. My reticence is not a projection of disrespect. Fear? Maybe. Indolence? Certainly not. *She seems nice enough*, I think as I sit awkwardly in the chair opposite hers. Other than the obligatory introductions to one another, not a word is being spoken. At least, nothing of real merit or substance. If there were a clock on the wall, I would undoubtedly hear the snapping seconds of its rotating hand.

It is not that she is unsure of what to say, nor is it that she is enjoying my discomfort; she is just giving me time. A nice thing to do, in retrospect. I won't lie; this is without a doubt the most unpleasant date I have ever been on.

Here I sit, hungover and sleep deprived, in a strange place with a woman I don't know, in a room soaked with silence, all against the backdrop of Valentine's Day. What a great date, indeed.

Thing is, I didn't schedule this meeting. Part of me doesn't think I need to be here, let alone stay. But I did come here today. And here I stay.

When enough wordless time passes, she interjects soft orations to elicit a verbal response from me. I find myself speaking one word, then another, and another after that. Before I know it, I am talking while looking at her through a wall of transparent tears that hug the lower lids of my weary eyes.

Valentine's Day is the occasion. The fourteenth is the day. The woman, a psychologist, and the quiet periods are apprehension. I continue cutting into the moments of silence with my quivering voice. My gaze lowers, but my words explain the reasons for my presence in her office. I open my mouth when prompted to do so and want to release *everything*. I think that if I share all of it she will give me some psychological incantation and I will be free of what ails me. This isn't the case.

I spend the better part of an hour just bleeding words. I tell her about my father and the abuse. I speak of my mother and her illnesses. I inform her of the boy. I throw tales of death, loss, rape, murder, suicide, and all manner of pernicious things at her. She absorbs them all. And when it is done, she informs me that we have only just begun.

I am given my diagnosis of PTSD and major depressive disorder almost immediately. I leave her office feeling punished and bewildered by the fact that I don't feel better. Naïve, I know. I am desperate—I want to be better—I want to get back on the ambulance and go back to work. But I am the patient now.

Full disclosure here—had it not been for the doc, had I not shown up for our "date," I would not be alive. Before I met Doc, I had a different date. It was a loathsome experience also—an experience that would see my feet swinging like a pendulum, high above a roadway as I sat dangling on the edge of an overpass. My mind was made up. I didn't bother writing or leaving a note—I hate suicide notes—all I had done to prepare for this date was ensure my bladder was empty and my stomach to match. I didn't want to be found with urine stains on my pants, a lesson I learned from the boy.

~

IT WAS THE DEAD OF night. The hot summer's air was sticky and dense, as though the world had opened its mouth and spewed condensation over everything. I sat on the railing of the overpass, allowing my feet to sway above the unsuspecting motorists below. I spoke introspectively, apologizing to my brother and my mum. I asked for forgiveness from my friends, my family, and those I had lost. I was at the stage where you plan two or three big breaths before initiating action. *One breath . . . two breaths . . . three . . . jump, Matt. Do it. It's the only way this ends. Just jump. It's better this way. You are nothing now. A fucking disgrace. Jump, you pussy, JUMP!*

I closed my eyes. I filled my nostrils with air. I could feel the damp inhalation cool as it slid along my tongue, dancing down my neck and in behind my collarbones before descending into my lungs. I was ready. I was going to jump now. I even felt my body begin to pull toward the roadway below. I opened my eyes for one last look at this wretched world. First to the horizon, then to the surface beneath. I inched closer. *Shimmy once, shimmy twice.* Palms were sweaty now. Heart was trying to flee the prison of my chest. It was time . . . All of a sudden, a flicker of light danced across the metal and plastic of an oncoming vehicle. My eyes tracked the ephemeral nictation—an ambulance—there was a passing ambulance about to scurry beneath me on its way to destinations unknown. They passed by without noticing me, but I noticed them—two young, fresh-faced medics in the front of the rig. I spun my head and followed the tail lights and watched as they grew smaller and more distant.

In one fluid motion, I pulled my overhanging legs up and over to the safe side of the banister and then collapsed with my back resting along the railing. My head and face fell into my hands, and I began to sob uncontrollably. I was alone, but alive. I chose not to end my life that night. Why? What stopped me from that last inch? The idea of becoming someone else's nightmare upon discovery. I thought of those young medics who had just passed beneath me, and I felt like a monster should I be the one who plagued their sleep the way my demons of loss haunt me. I stopped myself from jumping because I did not want to give someone else the motivation to follow in kind.

After that night on the bridge, I conceded to the idea of needing help. I initiated my employee benefits program and sought the interventions I so desperately needed. And by some miraculous twist of the universe, I found Doc. We have a Valentine's Day session today. It is neither lovely nor brief. But it is what saves me.

*Thanks, Doc.*

# CHAPTER 2

# Supermatt

MY EYELIDS CREEP UPWARD, UNVEILING the miserable start of a new day. A marching band passes through the chasms of my brain—hungover *again*. This is made worse by the fact that I can't stay in bed even if I want to. Today is therapy day. I have two choices: get my aching body out of bed and into the shower before making the trek to Doc's office, or phone and cancel, resulting in a self-administered injection of toxic thoughts about how stupid I am for doing so. Sadly, no matter which option I choose to lobby for, the end result will be beer in hand and whisky in the batter's box.

I decide to go. As I get my coat and lock the door to my apartment, I wonder, *How did I get to this point?*

I used to be a soldier, a medic, actually. A profession some may even consider valiant. I guess I always wanted to make a difference, help people, be a hero of sorts, even when I was a child.

~

WHEN I WAS A KID, I loved Superman! I did; I just did. As early as I can remember, I was drawn to the red and blue and always true man from Krypton. From the earliest age and from the first time my eyes saw that swirling red cape, I was hooked. Superman was my boy. Forget Batman or Spider-Man; it was all about the man who was faster than a speeding bullet.

I know without a doubt my love for Superman was real because of fragmented pieces of my memory—as well as begrudging testimonials from my older siblings and mother. At the age of four, I already knew my career path: I was going to *be* Superman. So much so that after watching *Superman* on VHS for the umpteenth time, I hopped to my feet and sprinted into the kitchen where my mum was having a cup of tea. With youthful vigour and effort, I leaped into the air and landed on one of the chairs.

"MATTHEW!" I heard my mum's sharp voice bellow.

"Mum! I am Superman. I need my costume; the city needs me!"

We were in England at the time. That's where I was born, so I likely spoke with an accent (let that sink in for a moment—a four-year-old boy with British inflections proclaiming he was Superman).

Some nights after being put to bed, I would roll onto my stomach and stretch my arms out in front of me, then mimic the noise of rushing wind from my mouth while pretending to fly through the air. Day or night, I was Superman.

I do not recall the day I received it, but I have vivid memories of the occasions when I would wear it. My dear mum made me an authentic red and blue outfit, complete with cape and little red underwear—she made me a Superman costume. Or better, she made *me* Superman. I wore that thing everywhere. In fact I would even sneak it underneath my day clothes when my mum was not looking. I remember one occasion when I was at a daycare while my mum was at work. The centre does not stand out in detail, but one quintessential element does: In one corner of the open-concept classroom, there was a replica phone booth. *Perfect*, I thought. When my adventurous eyes caught sight of this consummate structure, I knew what I had to do. I put down whatever childish toy I had been playing with, stood up, and then wandered over to the cardinal-coloured phone booth. The closer my little feet got to it, the more buttons I began undoing on my shirt. When close enough, I reached for the handle and slid inside, rushing to close the door behind me. I then began wiggling free from the constraints of my mild-mannered attire. Eventually "Matthew" was crumpled on the phone booth floor, and I emerged triumphant, clad from head to toe in flawless red and mesmerizing blue, cape and all. I had morphed into Superman.

I can't say that I remember the reactions of the other kids or the caregivers, but I do know that when my mum came to pick me up, she was stupefied at the sight of her superson. She had dropped me off earlier that morning without the knowledge I had hidden the cape and tights underneath my carefully selected wardrobe.

"Matthew? How did you get that on?"

"Mu . . . sorry . . . *Miss* . . . I do not know where Matthew is. I am Superman. I can help you find him!"

"Matthew, where are your clothes? NOW!"

"In the phone booth. Be right back." This was an event that would repeat itself on many occasions in a multitude of locations, much to the chagrin of my mum.

When Clark Kent hid around a corner or headed into a phone booth to become Superman, he removed his glasses, and he became even more handsome and captivating. When I removed my glasses, I became blind. No exaggeration. I could see nothing. My eyes were bad and my prescription strong. But you couldn't be a superhero and wear glasses. That was just madness. So I would often remove my spectacles, leaving them in locations I was doomed to forget. Nonetheless, I, the hero, would suit up and proceed to keep whatever dwelling I was within safe. I would fight a plethora of bad guys through my mind's eye. Oftentimes my pillow took the form of Lex Luthor and received a beating from Supermatt. It, or rather *he*, would be flung down the stairs, and I would be in hot pursuit.

I was always on the lookout for kryptonite, though. For me (a blind superhero), kryptonite often came in the form of table corners or slightly overturned rugs: SLAM! CRACK! SMASH!

"Matthew! Stop running into everything."

"Sorry, Mum. It was Lex."

I was never badly hurt, though. Until the day I was. On one morning after waking up, I ran to the bathroom. I had to pee. And I likely did so with the accuracy of an out-of-control sprinkler, irrigating all over the seat. No time to waste, though. Lex was around somewhere. I just knew it! I went back into my room and withdrew the handcrafted uniform from my drawer. My mother did a near perfect job. I was now decked out in my superattire and ready to tackle the nefarious deeds of any baddy.

I ran downstairs and barrelled into the TV room. My sister was on the couch watching something on the telly. Caring little for her comfort, or her ability to hear the show over my ongoing battle with the imaginary evildoers, I ducked in behind the couch. The couch in the family room was in front of a radiator. I learned that if I placed one hand onto the radiator (if it wasn't too hot) and placed the other onto the back of the couch, I could hoist myself off the ground and into the air, pretending I was flying upward and beyond. I grasped both the radiator and the couch and straightened my arms and took flight. Once again, the sounds of rushing air emitted from my mouth. Looking back on it, that annoyance is likely what led my sister to remove herself from the couch to seek refuge in another room, away from her pesky super-brother. However, when she got up from the couch, the weight of my tiny, little superbody was too much for the cushioned apparatus; it began to tilt backward and with that sudden shift, my flight was over. I plummeted to the ground below, and with a cacophonous BOOM, that couch made of kryptonite landed on top of my arm and shoulder. The sinister will of the couch broke my collarbone in two.

Now drained of my superpowers, I got to my feet and let loose a wail of agony any parent can decipher within seconds; something was wrong. I ran into the kitchen to find my mum. I was not wearing my glasses (of course), so I bounced off a wall here and there along the way.

My Superman days were over. Well, at least for the next four to six weeks.

Even though I retired my red cape that day, my desire to do something with purpose was still very much at work. Within a year or so of this incident, my family relocated to Canada, a country I would call my own and a land for which I would sign up to serve.

CHAPTER 3

# Shame

I STAND UP AND GRAB my jacket. I am not in the mood to say anything else, but I manage a polite head nod and goodbye. Doc replies in kind. "Don't forget next week's session," she reminds.

I am depleted: tired, frustrated, ashamed, and embarrassed—typical of how I leave a lot of my sessions with Doc, no fault of hers.

I slink past the waiting room and into the reverberant hallway of the building. I press the button to the elevator and wait. I hate myself in this moment. I despise myself for what we discussed and for knowing that it is all true. For me, it all acts as a further reminder as to what kind of dirtbag I really am. Doc assures me otherwise, but I dismiss her efforts by way of categorizing them into "obligatory musts." I can't even comprehend she might be sincere with her rebuking of my self-deprecating narrative. Especially after what I told her.

I take the elevator downstairs. I am happy to leave, but I am *not* happy. I take a moment to zip up my jacket and mentally prepare for the bus ride home—like working myself up for the big game.

The wind snaps and snarls its way down the busy street. As I approach the shanty-like bus stop, each passing car reminds me of my previous independence that I did not fully appreciate until I lost it. Once inside, I wait for my ride. My thoughts scurry, matching pace with the blustery weather. For me, the bus is not a convenience—it is a consequence. I have been given permission to drive since that day; I just don't—I won't.

The bus arrives, and I board the hefty caterpillar. I find a spot near the rear and settle in for my trip. I hate the bus—there are so many smells, sounds, and people. It can be overwhelming. But this is my prison sentence—self-imposed or otherwise.

I keep thinking about it. No matter how hard I try to push the negative thoughts back, they trundle to the forefront of my mind. The passing police cruiser outside my window does little to promote respite from weary introspection. As the wheels on the bus turn, my thoughts follow suit.

~

It was June, a few years back. A hot, humid night in summer. I had left work early to go and meet a friend for a beverage (or six). The bar he had selected was a few kilometres outside the city limits, a dingy little roadhouse, complete with rows of motorcycles out front. As I parked my car and started my way toward the aging brick and wood structure, I could hear the muffled sounds of jukebox music escaping from the inside: John Lee Hooker's "Boom Boom."

I pried back the dirty glass doors and pushed my way in. Inside was a jovial chaos—darts and pool, shots and whisky. My kind of place. I could see the rear profile of my buddy at the bar. I walked over, greeting my friend with a firm yet friendly hand slap to his shoulder—the night had officially begun.

"Hi, guys. My name is Nikki. What can I get ya?" the woman behind the bar asked.

"I'll take a Scotch. Eighteen-year, please."

"You have refined taste," she commented.

My gaze lingered as I responded. "Yes, I believe sometimes I do."

Nikki smiled and walked away. My buddy, Magic, a fellow medic, and I began conversing. We shared a lot of laughs and alcohol throughout the night, talking about all the silly calls we had been to as medics: There was the nineteen-year-old who called because he thought snakes were in his apartment. There weren't any. He was just high. Then there was frequent flyer Lady Grabby, a prolific user of the ambulance service, and a lady with overly friendly hands who enjoyed a good grab at the unsuspecting medic.

"Dude, do you remember the guy with the dog?"

"THE GUY WITH THE DOG!" Raucous laughter ensued.

Nikki floated in and out of our conversation, drinks in hand. She was kind and appeared to be interested, not in a rehearsed way—genuine. The bar may have been busy, but she was able to make us feel valued, asking questions about our careers. Her sincerity was impossible not to notice.

The eventual and inevitable last call rang through to the despondent crowd. Magic and I procured our last beverages of the evening. I will admit, my usual thoughts of trauma and pain had fallen victim to the numbing intoxication of a whisky venom—this was the desired effect alcohol played in my life. Outside all the funny calls we reminisced upon, there were the calls we never talked about—the bad ones. Those were the ones we needed to drink away—or so I thought.

The music had now been quieted and the chairs were being overturned onto tables. It was time to leave. I finished what was in my glass and went up to the bar to pay the tab. Using the well-worn edges of the bar-top as a leaning post, I waited for my bill to come. And it did. Nikki handed me the slip of paper as well as a kind smile. I looked down at it and noticed there was no black computer ink to be seen. Confused at first, I squinted to better bring it into focus. To my surprise, there was something written on the paper itself—blue ink scrawled on the back side of the slip: *Nice meeting you! Gimme a call sometime. I'd love to hear some of those funny stories you have,* followed by a number. Taken aback, I questioned the reality of my situation. I needed to confirm I wasn't seeing things. I politely beckoned for the beauty to return to the beast.

"Hey, 'sthis your number?"

"Haha. Yes. Call me! I gotta get to closing."

It was real. She gave me her number. A smile wiggled its way across my inebriated face. I folded the slip of paper and placed it into my pocket. Magic stood at the door, talking to a group of ladies whom he had befriended at some point in the evening. "Henny! We are going to get falafels. Wanna come?"

"Nah, man. I am good, thanks. I am gonna head home and get some sleep—gotta work tomorrow." I wasn't lying. I did have to work, but mostly I was done with being around people for now. We said our goodbyes and parted ways. I stepped out of the bar and into the sticky summer-night air. I walked with purpose toward my car and readied myself to drive home.

I placed the key into the ignition, sparking the roaring engine to life. I withdrew myself from my parking spot and turned onto the roadway. One left, then another, and before I could go any farther, my eyes became aware of a flickering in my rear-view mirror. It was almost blinding, certainly sobering: a police vehicle. I went from drunk to sober within the span of one failed gasp.

I pulled my car to the shoulder and parked along the curb. When the police vehicle followed in kind, I knew that the flashing red and blue was meant for me. I also knew what was about to happen. I was under no illusion that I was good to drive. I wasn't— no matter how seasoned I was.

I removed the keys from the ignition, threw them on the dashboard, and lowered my window. Before the police officer arrived at my car, I watched his silhouette grow in size and proximity in my rear-view mirror. I wasn't panicked, but my stoic demeanour wasn't forged from confidence, either. What I was experiencing was acceptance. I knew what I had done, and I knew what was going to be done.

I turned my head to meet the officer who was now standing at my window. A brief and cordial conversation took place, and I was asked how much I had to drink.

"No less than three, sir."

"Can you step out for me? I need you to perform a test."

"Yes, sir."

I removed myself from my vehicle, stood at the rear of my car, and blew into a machine, an act I have seen performed on a multitude of occasions when working as a medic. As I did so, my mind suddenly and mercilessly began to berate me with images and sounds of all the drunk crashes I had responded to as a paramedic. From behind my eyes, I could see bloodied faces. My ears recalled shrill screams and deafening pleas of pain and anguish. I was now standing in the footprints of a criminal—the tread of those footprints belonged to me. *What had I done?*

I failed the test. I was handcuffed and walked to the back of the police officer's SUV. I felt a hand on my head lower me, coaxing me into the back seat. On that muggy June night, the medic within me left—it couldn't stand the sight of me. Such a horrible thing: seeing your eyes peer back at you in the reflection of a police vehicle's rear-view mirror.

I would like to tell you that this was the day I became sober—it wasn't. It was, however, the first step to becoming a finger-printed criminal.

Months later, I would stand in court without representation or a trial. I would declare I was guilty. I was vehement about my sentencing. The judge tried to convince me to hold my plea and seek legal guidance—I didn't need a lawyer to inform me of my broken morality. Of that, I passed judgment on myself. I remained firm in my assertion of guilt. I was handed a two-year ban from driving and a criminal record. My paramedic's licence faded to dust as my driver's licence was relinquished in court.

From that point onward, I took the bus, a symbol of choice versus consequence. I never did call Nikki. I threw out the paper with her number the morning after I was arrested. She met a paramedic; I was now a criminal.

~

TODAY, AS I GET OFF the bus and head toward my apartment, I realize I probably shouldn't have left therapy early. I find the sessions about my childhood among the most fatiguing. I'm not sure if that's because the substance of what we are discussing is so weighted and heavy, or because I have spent a lifetime burying those experiences deep inside me, hoping they will simply disappear. They don't.

I unlock my door and collapse into a heap of despondency on my couch. My bachelor apartment affords me a certain amount of anonymity, blending into the fabric of urban Ontario, a far cry from my childhood home.

~

I GREW UP IN A small town in Western Canada, a sleepy little place you may miss if you happen to blink for long enough while passing by. It was a beautiful hamlet, carved deep in a mountain glen and nestled gently into the banks of a pristine lake, which often gave the illusion of being glass. The only reminder it was a living body of water came in the form of fish kisses poking the surface every now and then. In the summer, it was a little different: congeries of houseboats and kayaks floating indolently along the top of the lake, lovers walking hand in hand along the planks of the pier, excited children darting in and out of the way of lumbering adults, racing to see who could get to the end of the wharf first. A busy place, but laughable when compared to most urban sprawls. A perfect little town, but not without its contrasts—an idyllic backdrop to my tumultuous formative years.

One particularly bright day in the early fall stands out in my memory. It was a day when the waning summer's warmth refused to give way to the coming autumn weather. On my way home from school, I traipsed up a hill, allowing my distracted eyes to wander to this and that. The towering evergreens sheathed a gaggle of harmonic birds. It was a perfect day to be outside. Despite being newly released from the bonds of school, I was in no hurry to run home. Even though the hill leading to my place was a steep incline that seemed to ascend forever, my nine-year-old self had an endless supply of vigour and zeal.

As I continued to walk, I nibbled at the sandwich I hadn't eaten during lunchtime. In the security of my little town, the sight of a lone nine-year-old wandering from school to home was not unusual, so no one paid any attention to me. This gave my robust imagination time to ignite. In my mind's eye, there were enemy soldiers tucked secretively away in the treeline just ahead of me. As such, I dove to my right, sliding down the leaf- and twig-coated embankment and into the ravine. I picked up a stick that, when held in my hands, transformed into an M1921 Thompson submachine gun, complete with forearm vertical grip. With weapon securely held in hand, my pursed lips imitated the staccato pops of this iconic weapon.

*Dakka, dakka, dakka! Eat lead!* I waged war on my fictitious enemies and moved from cover to cover, even throwing my sandwich, which had transposed itself into a live grenade—*BOOM!* Before I knew it, I had reached a clearing and began ascending another wilderness-stricken slope. Branches, dirt, and twigs all gave way beneath my scurrying footfalls. I had reached the road—victory!

I could now see home base (my house). I threw my trusty stick gun onto the ground and began walking with determination toward the rear door of my house. I had already planned out what I was going to do once inside: remove the cumbersome backpack, kick off my footwear, head up the steps leading into the living area of our home, grab a tea, and then watch some TV—hopefully wrestling.

I reached up, twisted the glossy metal doorknob, and made my way inside. From there, I proceeded to implement my youthful plan. First, the bag was dropped from my shoulders, then, one shoe was kicked off in a direction unknown, then the second. I was now bounding up the stairs, skipping every other step. When I got to the top, I was startled by an unexpected sight—my mum, my sister, and two men dressed in police regalia, real guns and all.

I knew something wasn't right; I just had no idea what. The room felt heavy, and the innocence of being a kid evaporated faster than my plans.

"Matty," my mum said softly. Once I was able to tear my eyes away from the handguns on the hips of the police officers, I looked up to see my mother crying. Her face was red and puffy.

"Come, come sit by Mum, yeah?" I obliged, almost hypnotically. My mother's hand coaxed me over toward the loveseat where she sat. I folded my shaking little-boy legs and took a seat on the floor—my eyes returned to the holstered weapons on the officers' hips.

"Matthew . . . Mum's got some news, okay? It's bad news—your father has done something rotten. He won't be coming home . . . the police have taken him away."

My tiny ears received and ingested my mother's sombre words. However, digesting their ramifications became problematic—*What do you mean "my dad is gone"? What did he do?*

I looked away from the police and once again toward my mum. I asked that exact query. She responded through emotional hiccups and tear-stained words. She relayed to me that my father had harmed our family. She said he had done something illegal and that she had just found out about it and had to call the police—hence the two armed uniforms standing in my living room.

"My dad's gone? Can I see him? Why did he hurt us?" These questions went unanswered, my mother too upset to respond. I then turned my gaze upward toward the towering, authoritative men. My eyes re-sent the inquiry. They remained reticent and stoic. I could now feel an unsatisfying warmth boil from in behind my eyes. I was about to cry, and I was helpless in fighting my tears when I heard my mother gasp for air between bouts of grief.

My father, the figure who was supposed to teach me the intricacies of manhood, left me on a perfectly warm day at the start of autumn. I was nine on the morning I last saw him, and I was nine on the afternoon when I was told I would never see him again—

and I never did. I was left with a permanent reminder of him, however—a souvenir of sorts—a craggy scar on my lower back. I can't recall if it was spilled milk or a misspelled word. Either way, apparently it was *my* fault.

When I was nine years old, I won a fictitious war in the forest outside my home and lost my father, all in the span of one afternoon. There is still a battle that rages inside me—on one side, I have the axis of evil: guilt, shame, and embarrassment. And on the other side, I have the allies: forgiveness, self-compassion, and healing. I am still struggling to negotiate an armistice.

~

CURRENTLY, IN MY APARTMENT, THE fatigue of the day pulls me deeper into my couch, as if I have gone twelve rounds with Tyson. Though my skin is not bruised or broken, my spirit is down for the count. I fall asleep for a little while, only to be woken by ruminating thoughts, once again berating myself. Even though the judge's two-year sentence is long over and my father can no longer hurt me, I assume their punitive roles. I become my own abuser, flagellating myself with unforgiveness and self-loathing. Because that is what shame can do.

## CHAPTER 4

# Sentry

I DECIDE TO GO OUTSIDE. I have been sick for the past three days and need to get out of my apartment. I wander about for a while with no clear destination, ears protected by earphones that play nothing, muting the busy world around me, and sunglasses affording me a sense of anonymity. I grab a tea with honey from a local coffee shop. The day is going well.

I am hungry, so I wander into a pub I typically frequent. Inside, I find a plethora of distractions. I sit down and order a beer.

~

I WAS TWELVE YEARS OLD when I first realized my weekends away from school were a little different from those of my peers. Sure, I got to play the latest video game or head outside and shoot the puck around for a while like any other kid, but there was something else I did that seemed different—sit in the family bathroom beside a woman dying of cancer. The woman? My mother. When I was young and sometime after the sinister departure of my father, my mum became stricken with the evil disease. The big C. This meant I grew accustomed to seeing her embraced by oxygen tubing and intravenous lines, surrounded by a swath of beeping machines while she lay in a hospital bed.

Sometimes, and much to her chagrin, I would leave school early, bringing my homework with me to go sit in her hospital room for a while. There were times when, to a young boy, it felt as though she was always gone, so I would do what I could to be nearer to her. When she was home, she was still battling the effects of chemotherapy. This crusade usually consisted of multiple visits to the bathroom. When I was in my bedroom, I could hear her muffled grunts and groans pushing past the wall as she struggled to rid herself of the poison. At night, when I closed my eyes, I could see two versions of my mum: One was beautiful and happy, smiling and strong. She had all the answers, and I was safe in her presence. The other, a frail woman who had aged decades in the span of mere moments, a woman whose hair was beginning to grey and fall. Strands escaped her scalp like leaves from an autumn tree. I knew this because there were times when I grew weary of hearing her lonesome struggle, and I would invite myself into the bathroom, sit beside her on the bathtub, and try to hold her hair back from her wincing face. When all was said and done during those times, I was left holding straw-like strands of my mother's fleeting hair.

I was always in awe of my mother's resiliency. No matter how hard the disease hit her, she fought back. Although I was twelve years old when I knew that weekends were different for me, I was also twelve years old when I was gifted a firsthand look at what untamed courage really looks like—an incredible sight.

Amidst my mother's unrivalled tenacity, there were moments of humility and solemn requests—times when my mother was so afraid to fall asleep, she would ask me to sit outside of her door until she was able to rest.

"Matt, keep the door open, yeah? Sit for a while, could you?"

"Sure, Mum . . . I guess." I was young. I thought I had better things to do, but part of me was humbled to be considered for the job. I would close the door a ways and then sit in the hallway just outside her room. These times often felt unforgivably long to my adolescent brain. But part of me held a maturity beyond my years, thrust upon me by the hands of an absent father, a fractured family, and a critically ill mother. So I would be a faithful sentry, and I would sit and wait.

I became good at living in my head. I also became proficient at reading, something I would often do when waiting for my mother to fall into a deep-enough sleep so I could leave my post. The topics I would visit in my mind were varied and diverse. I would think about a homework assignment I had let lapse to the last moment, dooming me to receive late marks upon its eventual turn-in. I would ponder what had happened on the latest episode of *WWE Monday Night Raw*. I would also think about girls—I was helplessly seduced and vexed by them from day one. There was one in particular at my school, Mia. She was beautiful. The kind of pretty that made a boy's stomach uneasy and excited. Before allowing myself to dive too far into the delightful rumination, I would often cast a glimpse over my shoulder in through the cracked door to my mother on her bed. I could usually tell when she had fallen asleep by the way she was breathing—or snoring. My mother had an award-winning snore.

Mia was the first girl I ever spoke to my mum about. I didn't have a dad, so Mum would have to do. I went to her one day, telling her of this pretty girl in my class. I spoke every word through a foolish smile. My mother, bless her soul, sick as a dog, managed to put up with my monologue of romance about a girl who had no idea I existed.

"Mum, you gotta see this girl . . . She's got this hair and her smile, oh, and the way she bites onto a chip package before opening it . . . she's amazing!" My mother, resting on the couch, smiled and responded, "She sounds lovely, Matty. You go ask her out. Tell her 'Mum said so.'" Another smile, and then she closed her tired eyes.

*Yeah, ask her out . . . That's exactly what I have to do!*

I ran to my room and began pacing across every carpeted square inch, trying to figure out how. I must have looked like a mad scientist who wore a boyish heart on his sleeve. My mind darted from one idea to the next. I had to get this right—she was worth it. I began taking inventory of all the things I had seen her do and enjoy while at school: *She likes biting the ends of pencils. I could get her some really expensive pencils! No, that's dumb. She likes Swedish Berries. Yeah, get her some candy!* I ran over to my ceramic piggy-bank—thirteen cents, some lint, and a Hubba Bubba gum wrapper?! Shit . . . Now resembling Winnie the Pooh when he was deep in thought about honey, I continued to think about what I could possibly do to win over this unblemished beauty of my Grade 5 class. And that's when it hit me—Winnie the Pooh . . . cartoons. *Matt, you can draw. Draw her a cartoon of you asking her out. Cha-ching!* Plan made.

I dove into my reading desk and withdrew a pad of paper and a pencil. Holding the pencil like Arthur held the sword, I got to work right away. I drew a line or two, then ripped the page from its bindings and angrily crumpled it before tossing it over my shoulder and onto the floor. A process that occurred with some repetition—too much repetition, actually. But eventually I was successful. I had managed to draw a cartoon facsimile of both me and a girl meant to be Mia. My cartoon self was festooned with a shirt and tie, sported dapper slacks, and held a bouquet of roses outstretched for the young lady. Written within a speech bubble was the text: Mia, *do you want to go out sometime? Yes. No. Maybe?*

I sat back in my wobbly desk chair and examined the hand-crafted masterpiece of love. A smile shimmied its way to one side of my mouth. This had to work. Knowing I was not your traditional staple of handsome, I had to step it up a bit. I could not get away with simply wearing a Ninja Turtle T-shirt and a pair of jeans when performing this act. So into my closet I went. I grew the remaining six arms of an octopus and began hastily slinging clothes from their hangers and discarding the unwanted and unworthy to the floor behind me.

I would eventually find something I deemed acceptable for this endeavour—a plain white T-shirt, a pair of crinkle-free khakis, and a sweater vest. Yes, a sweater vest.

I carefully laid out the selected outfit and put myself to bed, but only after checking on my mum. I crawled into my bed and began rehearsing what I was going to say to Mia. I may have been merely a boy, but in my head I sounded like Tom Selleck, moustache and all.

Eventually, I was able to fall asleep. When morning came, I leaped from my bed and began readying for the momentous day at hand. I, of course, checked up on Mum—she was resting. In the act of getting everything just right, I even went into the bathroom and used some of my brother's cologne. *Too much, I used too much. Whatever, can't take it off now.* I finished getting ready and made my way to school.

It was a crisp fall morning, the grass coated in a thick blanket of morning dew. The clouds parted like curtains in the sky, revealing a brilliant orange glow of the new day's sun. Birds were still singing, albeit not as vibrantly as they had been a few months prior.

Once at school, I took my seat and began to scan the room for Mia. She hadn't arrived yet. I began to worry that she may not show. But just as quickly as that fleeting worry came and went, Mia wandered in and took her seat near the front of the class. She looked exquisite that morning. Mrs. Applebaum, our teacher, droned on for what felt like an eternity. Every time I threw a glance toward the clock, the second hand appeared to stop counting and remain motionless.

The time came, though. The bell finally chimed, and we were set loose for lunch hour. I knew Mia would likely go outside with her entourage of girls and sit in the ball diamond. If I was going to pull this off, it had to be there. I knew there was no way to get her alone, so I conversed with myself, attempting to evoke some form of unknown bravery.

I grabbed my bag and went outside. I sat on the lower half of the bleachers just off to the right of the ball field. I was correct. Mia emerged soon thereafter along with her group of friends. This was it, now or never. I waited for her to get to her usual spot and settle in for lunch. I thought this was the polite thing to do. It was also because I was scared shitless about what was about to happen.

Beads of sweat had now formed a crown around my scalp, and one by one they trickled from hairline to chin—I was shaking. No matter, this had to be done. Mum said so.

I mustered up what little courage I could and yelled inside myself, demanding my feet to move forward. They apprehensively obliged. I walked past the gates and onto the grass of the baseball field. I could hear my feet sift through the blades of grass as I neared Mia—home plate.

"Hey . . . uh, Mia." She stopped what she was doing and looked up at me, using her hand to shield those big brown eyes from a hanging sun.

"Yeah?"

"Hey—uh, I—uh, this, this is for you." I extended my hand and presented her with the meticulously folded piece of paper.

"Me? What even is it?"

"Uh—it's, it's for you." Laughter exploded from all except me.

"Okay . . . Thanks."

"Oh, yeah. No worries. Have a good rest of your lunch day." *What the hell did I just say?*

Dejected, I hurried away. I retreated back to the sanctuary of the lower bleachers. By now I could see that Mia had unfolded the slip of paper. She was holding it in her hands, and her friends all stood behind her, peering over her shoulders. If I had to guess if her friends played the part of the angel or the devil on her shoulder—well, my money would not have been on the angel.

I saw a smile come to her face. A real, genuine smile. She peeked up from the page and began hunting for me with her eyes. She looked left then right, and then we caught one another from across the grassy field. She was still smiling. I was twisted with anxious anticipation. Nervously I pulled my gaze away from her, pretending I was disinterested in what was going on. I was trying to play it cool.

As I peered over to the roadway, my right ear snagged the sound of laughter. Not slight nor subtle—uproarious. Mia and her friends had devolved into deep guffaws at my expense. Mia began showing any—and all—passersby the doodle. She even pointed over to me to show them who was responsible for this unexpected hilarity. I watched as she let the note descend from her hands and onto the red-stoned gravel of the ball diamond. Once it had fallen, she used her foot to grind it into home plate. The only time in history that home plate was not a place of victory.

There was no *yes, no, maybe* selected. But I was able to deduce the answer was a firm no. I survived some light teasing for the rest of the day and then made my way home. Mum was on the couch again. She never asked me about Mia or how it went, so I was spared the embarrassment of telling her I had failed. Instead, I just sat with her for a while—both of us despondent, but for vastly different reasons. I, for one, blamed the sweater vest.

That was how a lot of my youth was spent. Moments of awkwardness and horrible sadness. Of course, it wasn't all bad—my mum beat cancer's ass! That's a pretty big win.

Mia wouldn't be my only unsettling romance. Many years later, as an adult in my late twenties, I would take a hockey stick to the windows of my truck; better to administer anger onto an inanimate object than onto a living being. Unlike my twelve-year-old self, I could no longer sit guard at the bedroom door. Eventually I gained the courage to leave a seven-year relationship that was no longer functioning. Soldiering on in that union was not healthy for me, so I quit my job, packed what I could into my Ford Fusion, and drove cross-country from western Canada to Ontario, hardly knowing a soul and with no career secured.

~

SO HERE I SIT. IN a pub. Thousands of kilometres from my previous life. For so long, I stood on guard for my mum, my relationship, and my country. Now I simply protect my seat at the bar, feeling more "false, directionless, weak, and shackled" than "true, north, strong, and free."

"Hey, there, you want another?"

*Yes. No. Maybe?*

"Yes, please. And another after that, too."

# CHAPTER 5

# Challenging Narratives

ALL I CAN HEAR IS the sound of my nervous breathing, emotions simmering beneath the surface of my skin. I open my mouth and speak. "Doc, I didn't deploy. How can I have PTSD?"

She politely stops me and interjects. "Many soldiers who were never deployed have service injuries. Trauma isn't limited solely to deployment." I remain resistant to her thoughtful and professional opinions. I feel guilty. After all, I am alive. Many of my friends are not.

My sessions challenge my narrative of what it means to be injured. A soldier—that is what I used to be.

~

ALTHOUGH NOT THE MOMENT I first made my career choice, the day the towers fell cemented the idea. My eyes refused to blink or move. Beside me stood my mother. Her hand covered her mouth in worry and wait. Up to that point in my young life, images such as these had been reserved for the latest summer blockbuster. Works of fiction. I was hypnotized by the reality of it all. That day was September 11, 2001. A month prior, I had expressed to my mother my interest in joining the army. Now, we both stood motionless, watching the world fall apart. I hadn't wavered in my conviction to serve, though. If anything, this sparked a youthful and naïve bravado toward that service.

In the days that followed that fateful Tuesday morning, my mother mentioned I might want to reconsider joining the forces. I heard what she had to say, but it did little to dissuade me. My decision to join and to serve was born long before that abhorrent day in September.

The moment I knew I was going to be a soldier happened years before, actually. I was in my room, staring at my reading book and homework assignment, dreading the boring passages of text I was about to study. I glanced toward the television, and something caught my eye—a news ticker-bar displayed at the bottom of the screen. It read: Breaking News—War in Serbia.

I watched as images of firebombed buildings were tossed onto the screen. It appeared to be chaos and madness. In the background of all passing shots of combat footage, blankets of thick, pluming smoke billowed into the distance. As if that were not captivating enough to a sombre eye, I found something else to fixate on—an image of a lone soldier, holding a weapon while wearing a red cross.

He looked like a medic, but he was carrying a gun. I had never known medics to carry weapons. All the books and texts I had read indicated they were not to shoot or to be shot at. Their job was to help the injured and dying. And that was true, for a while. But times had changed and so had warfare—as I was beginning to learn.

Homework took a back seat to intrigue that night, and I began to formulate a plan: I was going to use the school library and find out how it was possible that a medic could be carrying a weapon and still be helping the wounded. The kind librarian assisted me with this task. At the school, there were some brochures from the Canadian Armed Forces that explained job descriptions and titles. They seemed to cover all aspects of the military except the position of medic. Everywhere I looked, there was nothing but outdated or skeletal information about the famed position.

I somehow got it into my head I had to join as an infantry soldier and then request to have specialized medical training—not sure why, but that made sense to me back then. As such, I begged my older brother Jon to give me a ride to the nearest recruiting centre the summer after I had graduated high school, so I could inquire about enlisting. He took a day off work and gave me a ride. It was a beautiful summer day. Growing up in BC, that was not a rarity—but it was appreciated every time.

At the recruiting centre, I sat down with an officer and unleashed my excitement and desires. She smiled and tolerated my zeal. She told me I would have to undergo strict physical and intellectual testing before she could inform me of what job I was best fitted for. I did not mind, nor did I pay her words much attention. I already knew what I was going to do—become infantry and then specialize in combat medicine. That red cross was going to be mine.

Several weeks later, I was called back to the recruiting centre to learn the results of my various tests. It was pouring that day, hard. As I sat in the chair across from the female officer, I could hear the rain smack the window behind me. It sounded like a toddler playing the drums. I watched her as she used her stern gaze, scrutinizing my scores. She closed the folder and then looked up at me, my face likely displaying a mixture of childish glee and forbearance. As she began to speak, I started to understand the news she had for me was not good. I could hear it in her voice, and those serious, disciplined eyes had melted into an empathetic stare.

"Mr. Heneghan, your scores are all very good. You did quite well, and we are happy to have your interest. However . . ."

*Wait, what? However? However?! That's bad—however is always bad.* "I do have some unfortunate news regarding your medical: Matthew, your eyesight does not allow for you to apply nor qualify for any of the combat arms trades . . . you cannot be infantry."

"I can't?"

"No. I'm afraid not."

The storm outside suddenly felt befitting of how my day was turning out to be.

"So I can't be a soldier?"

"Well, everyone in the army is considered a soldier first, but what I am saying is that you cannot be in the combat arms . . . you can't be an infantry soldier. We do have some excellent support roles you are suited . . ."

I began to speak, stopping the officer mid-sentence. "Um, no. I mean, wait. So I can't join the army?"

"No, you can. It's just not as an infantryman. Here, look at these." She slid a pile of pamphlets over to me. My eyes instantly recognized them—I had already seen these in my school library. I was crushed—defeated and dejected. My plan, my life, it had all just fallen apart, much like the towers would months from that day.

I politely accepted the pamphlets and skulked over to the waiting room chairs. I sat down and tossed the flyers onto an empty seat beside me, an act the officer must have seen. She floated over to me and knelt into view.

"Here, some water. I have a video I'd like to show you. You said you want front-line work. I think I may have something. Come, please."

With a heavy heart, I obliged. She walked me into a quiet area of the recruitment station and sat me down in front of a TV. She placed a DVD inside the machine and pressed PLAY. She smiled at me subtly and walked away leaving me with some privacy. The video started playing, and my eyes began to widen and fixate once more. There on the screen was a soldier—a soldier with a red cross and a rifle. The medic. I watched the video through to the end and then peered back at the officer. She walked over to me with a leaflet in hand, a brochure that I had not yet seen, a folded slip of shiny, wax-like paper. All the information I would need about the combat medic. Turns out, I did not need to be an infantryman to become a medic—I just needed to become a medic. And that's exactly what I did.

In January of 2002, I was on a plane hurdling toward Quebec to begin basic training. A ten-week adventure that would chip away the civilian and replace that indolence with discipline and pride. Step one to becoming a soldier.

Over the course of that ten-week nightmare, I would learn a lot about myself. I learned that I could scale six-foot walls with nothing more than a rope and some motivation. I rappelled from thirty-foot towers, walked over thirteen kilometres with a weighted rucksack and Kevlar, fired a rifle, and mastered its assembly and disassembly. I transformed from a nervous, awkward kid into a mature figure of stoicism and humility. I had become a Canadian soldier.

My mum and brother even flew out to see me graduate. They watched as I performed drills alongside my newly acquired brothers and sisters. In the evening time, I was allowed to have dinner with them off base. It was a fleeting visit but a nice one—a visit made more poignant for me by the fact that shortly afterward my mum stopped speaking to me for the duration of two years.

When I left home earlier to join the army, we had been residing in a subsidized three-bedroom home. My mother couldn't work; she was too sick. Besides having cancer once again, my mother suffered from a myriad of mental illnesses. We often had to rely on the fluctuating kindness of our government and small-town welfare system—not an easy way to grow up.

The lease was up for renewal while I was in Ontario training for my red cross. My mother was not able to tell the authorities when I would return home, if at all. As such, she was requested, well *told*, to relocate to another unit—a one-bedroom, meaning my brother was out of a place to live, too. My mum did not function well alone. So she did what she so often did: She devised a plan in her head and assumed that she had told us about it and that we agreed with her—a conversation we were always absent for.

My mother knew I had a steady job; She also knew my older brother was great with money and that he, too, worked full time. So she thought we should get together and buy a house. By the time I had learned of this master plan, my mother had already found a real estate agent, picked out a home, viewed it, liked it, wanted it, and said we would take it. Now, keep in mind, I was new to the army, meaning I was a private when all this was going down. I was not making bank. Not by a long shot. You don't join the army to become rich.

When my mother asked if I would co-sign a mortgage with my brother, I was apprehensive. So I declined. I just didn't have the money. My mother felt slighted by this. So she told me that she was going to kill herself, and when that did not work to sway me, she banished me from being on the family team, which meant the silent treatment. My mother was often not speaking to one or another of my siblings at any given time. It was now my turn to be relegated to the sidelines.

~

Now, like most other nights, I go to the bar. It seems like several lifetimes ago I was training to be a medic. I proceed to get absolutely crippling drunk. I loathe myself. I am alive and have all my limbs, eyesight, hearing, and touch, yet I am debilitated by my mind—I feel weak.

But Doc has challenged my claim of truth. Just like I thought medics couldn't bear arms, or my eyesight would prevent me from joining the army, or I had to be in the infantry before applying to be a medic, or my mother would never speak to me again, sometimes I got it wrong. Maybe I am not weak after all. Maybe I am injured. Not all injuries look the same. Embracing this new, more compassionate narrative is fleeting, however. I soon tumble back into the comfortable burden of my self-hatred.

I think about how deeply impacted I am by the great losses I experienced while in the Canadian Armed Forces until I drink enough that I can no longer think about anything at all. I am not sure how I do it in my paralytic state, but somehow I make it home to my apartment. A wounded soldier: left, right, left . . .

# CHAPTER 6

# Sting

It's 2:30 A.M., AND I wake with a start. My body is covered in a glistening sweat. I feel as though I should be standing at attention, listening to the deafening crack of rifle fire. After utilizing a few of the grounding techniques I have learned in therapy, I am able to reacclimate to the fact that I am home. The damage is done, though. My sheets are soiled with sweat, and my heart is running a marathon.

I continue to gather my thoughts from a groggy haze and make my way to the shower. The water cleans my body but does not erase the nightmare. *If only it were that easy.* I return to my bedroom, strip the bed of its linens, and place them into a laundry bag. My hands feel the damp fabric, saturated with my sweat.

I *had* been sleeping, but my slumber gave way to an uninvited intrusion from my PTSD brain. The sound of gunshots pierced their way through my ears and into my resting mind. The result—death of my sleep and a haunting clatter, which is all too familiar.

As I pack my laundry bag, I chastise my mind for replaying those unwanted nightmares. But it is useless. I replay, and most likely will continue to replay, those undesired flashbacks and horrible thoughts. *When will it end? Or worse, will it ever end?*

Part of me wants to break down and cry; the other part of me wants to grasp this newly filled laundry bag and heave it across the infinitesimal room—small in space but grandiose in meaning. It is the place where I am damned from finding rest. I choose neither option. Instead I swallow hard, pick up the laundry bag, sling it over my shoulder, and head out the door. I make it about halfway to the laundromat and realize it is closed. It doesn't open until 4:00 a.m. It is in this moment I let loose a frustrated shout into the night sky. I feel a heavy sense of defeat on my shoulders, which joins the weight of my laundry. I walk over to a local coffee shop still open at this hour and get a tea.

I go back to my apartment and look at my bed, which is now absent of sheets. I find myself having to sleep on the couch. Although I don't have an upset girlfriend to banish me there, I do have an angry, scarred enemy of a mind that showers me with punitive messages, exiling me to the same fate. Sometimes I wish I could transport myself back to an easier time, a time before nightmares and PTSD—a time when my mind would think about lighter, happier memories. The good stories. That is what I long for.

Now blessed with the gift of consciousness, I rack my brain for a pleasant recollection, anything to make me chuckle—or at the very least, smile. Then it comes to me, a story I have shared more than once to anyone who would give me audience. It occurred shortly after I had graduated from basic training.

~

I WAS TO BE ON a bus at zero-dark-stupid hour to head to Ontario where I would begin the next phase of my evolution—to get that red cross. Although I would get that cross, I wouldn't begin my training right away.

The younger me had a skeletal physique and a somewhat awkward configuration, nothing short of a greyhound. I had just finished basic training and was posted to a place called the Post Recruit Educational and Training Centre, or PRETC. The military loves acronyms. It was early in the morning, and the sun was hanging low in the orange sky. Already the excruciating heat of a looming summer day was making its way through the window. My bunkmates and I were sprawled on top of our thin military mattresses, waiting for the inevitable wake-up call to begin: PT (physical training). Conceding to the inescapable, I pried my sticky, sweat-lathered skin from the dampened sheets of the bed, sitting on its edge for a moment before reaching underneath to retrieve my running shoes. On a morning where the sun was already mocking us with its heat, we were due to go running. And run we did. We snaked in and out from running paths to biking lanes and back to sidewalks. The humidity surrounded us like a goddamn sauna.

Upon returning to the barracks from our miserable morning torture, I hastily made my way to the showers and began revelling in the cool streams of water spraying from the shower head. After finishing the shower and having a quick bite to eat, it was off to the warehouse: a giant metal structure that housed all of the senior non-commissioned officers as well as us—the stubble-headed baby troops. This was where we met each day and where, each day, the sergeants and master corporals would dish out daily assignments. The tasks could be anything from sweeping the same patch of spotless cement flooring until they said to stop to picking up the desks and moving them to an arbitrary location on the other side of the warehouse. One of the things they used to love to say was "repeat until successful," meaning don't ask if it's good enough. They'll tell you if it is, and they'll let you know when you're finished.

After the assignments had been doled out, I was left without a task, which meant I, along with the other unchosen, was to retreat to a section of the barren warehouse that was made up of some crudely erected office-styled cubicles. We were to sit there just in case anything should come up we may be needed for. I removed my beret, claimed a chair, and settled in for the long wait. Just as you would suspect, there were many days where there was nothing for us to do, so we just sat there. Sat there and counted the cracks in the blue-tinted pavement or tried to decipher the initials carved into the sides of the well-aged wooden desks while picturing who they once belonged to.

I was in the process of constructing a fable about someone with the initials CW when the metal roofing rattled with the sound of a sergeant's booming voice calling for me. I sprang up from my chair and rounded one of the cubicle walls to make myself visible to the hollering sergeant.

"HENEGHAN!" he demanded.

I stood tall and called back to ensure he knew I had heard his request for a specific private: "YES, SERGEANT!"

"ON ME. Double TIME!"

"YES, SERGEANT!"

I hustled over to where the statuesque sergeant stood waiting for me. I jogged until I was within about an arm's length and then came to a sudden stop while slamming my heel down to the pavement, assuming the position of attention. The clatter of my boot striking the cement flooring gave off a sudden and thunderous boom—the sound of discipline. It echoed faintly off the metal walls of the building while I stood at attention, awaiting further instruction from the stoic sergeant.

"Warrant wants to see you. Follow me."

"Yes, Sergeant."

My lanky arms and Gumby-like strides kept pace behind the solid gait of the sergeant. We were nearing the office where the platoon warrant was situated. I knew I had done nothing wrong, but my mind couldn't help fabricating possible scenarios. After all, it was not often that the warrant had the need of a face-to-face with a private.

As we got to a door frame void of a door itself, I was instructed to stop and stand at attention and wait outside. *What the hell did I do wrong?!* I won't lie; I was now sweating not only due to the ferocious summer heat but also due to fear, irrational or otherwise.

I stood as rigid as a post. My eyes found a fixed point on the wall across from me, and I bore a hole through it, refusing to blink. After what seemed like an infinitesimal amount of time, the sergeant reappeared in front of me. With his head slightly lowered so as to be able to lock eyes with me, he instructed me that the warrant was ready to see me now. I moved with purpose, discipline, and accuracy as I entered the office. Coming to a stop at the position of attention once more, I looked straight ahead of me. I could see the figure of the warrant at the bottom of my gaze, but I did not dare look down.

"Heneghan?"

"YES, WARRANT!"

"Jesus, don't yell. I have a headache . . . and a wife. She yells . . . my daughter, too."

Lowering my tone slightly, I responded once more. "Yes, Warrant."

"Heneghan, you're not tasked with anything today, are you?"

"No, Warrant."

"Tragedy. A soldier such as yourself should never be without direction or purpose. Let's fix this egregious oversight and misappropriation of resources, shall we?"

"Yes, Warrant."

"Out-fucking-standing. Follow me, Troop."

The warrant was a veteran in every sense of the word. He boasted a rust-coloured moustache on his upper lip, complete with the ends waxed and curled into hooks. It was also stained with the remains of the copious cigarettes he had inhaled throughout his long service to his country. Other than his rank and his appearance, none of the privates knew much about him, so he became more of a figure of lore handed down to the newly arriving recruits from the departing ones. By this time, I had heard my share of impossible tales regarding the warrant and his worldly exploits.

The warrant walked in front of me, not even bothering to throw a glance over his shoulder to ensure I was in tow. He knew I would be—and I was. We walked around the corner of the offices and down a dusty corridor festooned with flickering lighting high above us, hanging from time-worn beams. He led me to a side entrance that we privates dared not use—unless otherwise authorized. He leaned in with his left shoulder and hip, forcing the door to open. We exited the steel warehouse and walked into the unforgiving inferno outside.

"Jesus Christ, it is hotter than a sweatbox in Tijuana out here, Heneghan," the warrant bellowed out while retrieving a nearly empty pack of cigarettes from his front breast pocket.

While placing the white-covered tube of tobacco into his mouth, he spoke through pursed lips and said, "Heneghan, you know where your barracks are from here?" Feeling slightly confused by the question, I delayed in responding to his query.

"Heneghan, for the love of God, please tell me you know where you live."

"Yes, uh . . . yes, Warrant."

"Good. We're halfway there. Now, Heneghan, here's what I want you to do: I want you to, on the double, head back to your shack, go up to your room, take a shit if you want to, but what I need from you is this . . . grab your CBRN suit and gas mask with carrier, and come back to me. Understood?"

"Yes, Warrant."

By now the warrant had taken a few drags from his newly lit carcinogenic delight. Each time he spoke, plumes of bluish-grey smoke swirled behind his sarcastic delivery.

"Heneghan, didn't you hear what I said? Go, Troop, git."

"Shit, uh . . . yes, Warrant."

Like a runner who just heard the crack of a starter pistol, I took off, racing my way through the dense summer heat. It was so hot and muggy that taking a deep breath was almost impossible, lessening my ability to maintain the lightning-like pace I had started with. Now settling into a jog, I followed the winding path from the warehouse to the barracks, which was roughly a five- or ten-minute jaunt. But in this ungodly heat, they felt like they were miles apart.

After retrieving the requested and somewhat perplexing items from my kit bag in my room, I bounded down the stairs and, outside once again, I charged forward in a full-tilt sprint. I ran the same path as before and eventually made it back to the warehouse. Now drenched in sweat, I found myself standing outside the warrant's office—albeit a little more winded than I had been before. I was once again invited in, this time by the sound of the warrant's gruff baritone. Maybe he could smell me standing there. I entered and, as I did before, stood motionless at attention in front of his desk. He looked up at me and spoke with playful wit: "Heneghan, relax would ya. You're stressing me out. Relax, man. You look like you're wound tighter than a balloon knot, son." I apprehensively released the tension from my shoulders and stood slightly at ease.

"Heneghan, you know what the CBRN suit is used for, yes?"

"Yes, Warrant."

"Well, don't leave me in suspense, Troop. I'm an old man. I could stand here and die before you get a chance to tell me. What's it for?"

"Warrant, the CBRN suit is an issued piece of a soldier's essential kit intended to combat the effects and hazards of a chemical, biological, radiological, or nuclear attack from the enemy."

After a slight pause and a somewhat bewildered look that slithered across the warrant's face, he responded: "Well, yeah . . . I mean, we all know that . . . I mean I do *now*. Okay, all that *plus* . . . follow me. I'll show you."

I followed behind the warrant as he led me back through the narrow halls behind the offices. We made our way out into the smoker's area and stood together in the stifling heat. He capitalized on this location by reaching into his pocket and grabbing his vice from its foiled packet, another cigarette.

"Heneghan, MOPP 2, now."

This was the warrant's order to have me get into the insulated green standard-issue zip-up suit, designed to be worn in the event of some kind of nuclear war. Without wasting any time, I twitched into action and began grunting my way into this oversized onesie. MOPP 2 (or the second mission-oriented protective position) meant I was to physically wear everything minus the gas mask and the cumbersome rubber gloves. After dancing in place, I was finally dressed in what the warrant had ordered.

After looking at me with a subtle grin, he shouted, "GAS! GAS! GAS!"

This meant I was to systematically grab the gas mask from the carrier I was wearing around my waist and throw it on over my head and face in rapid time. In a real-life scenario, delay meant death. This was something we practised often. It's also a good way for non-commissioned officers to fuck with us troops. And I couldn't help but feel I was indeed being fucked with.

What a picture I must have been, a nervous and slightly awkwardly thin young man, standing outside in the devil's heat, clad from head to toe in an oversized green suit, which was intended to be worn only in the event of a nuclear or biological attack. It was complete with a standard-issue gas mask, which boasted bulbous eyepieces and a giant canister on one side of it, completely muffling my voice and severely limiting my ability to take in large amounts of air. Underneath the rubber and plastic mask I was sweating buckets, and my eyes were stinging because of it. I was miserable. I stood in front of the warrant as he continued to inhale from his lit cigarette with no haste at all. The fact that I was the only one standing around like we were being bombed seemed lost on him but not on those passing by.

"Heneghan, do you know what I hate? No, of course you don't. Forget I asked. I'll just tell you—Heneghan, what I hate is an enemy who exploits complacency and weakness within the ranks I control. I mean, I hate it. Makes me feel like I'm a bad warrant officer, and I don't much think I am. Do you? Heneghan, don't answer that right now . . ."

His speech went on for a while, and it resembled something out of a movie as he paced around on the spot, his hands now securely clasped behind his back. Only when he really wanted to get a point across or accentuate something did he release and use one of his hands to cut through the air like a musical conductor. His speech dragged and, to the best of my recollection, went on something like this: "So, Heneghan, now that we both agree I am not a bad warrant, and likely one of the best, you can understand why a sneaky enemy is so troublesome to me, can't you?"

I remained reticent, waiting for his monologue of rhetorical queries to continue.

"Heneghan, answer me. Can you see why?"

"Uh . . . yes, Warrant." My voice barely broke through the dense rubber insulation cupping my mouth. I likely sounded like a nervous Darth Vader if you can picture such a thing. Maybe think *Spaceballs*.

"Good! Okay, then. So you will also agree that, in the face of a sneaky enemy who is trying to exploit our weaknesses, a quick and concise counterattack would be prudent . . . and perhaps even effective in thwarting the enemy's foul intentions, yes?"

"Yes, Warrant."

"Heneghan, I can barely hear you, and it's as hot as a brothel in Da Nang out here. Not that I would know anything about that . . . a friend told me. Anyway, I am going to assume you are agreeing with what I am saying. If that's correct, nod your fuckin' dome."

I did.

"Good. Heneghan, ABOUT TURN!"

This was the order to quickly spin around 180 degrees. In one skillful motion, I spun around and was confronted by the blank metal outer wall of the warehouse.

"Heneghan, I want you to relax a little, and I want you to look up."

I complied with his request, but it didn't help that the relentless sweat was crippling my eyes from behind the mask.

"Heneghan, I want you to scan the ledge where the roof meets the wall. Seen?"

"Seen, Warrant."

"Good. Now follow that line to your left until you see the relatively low-hanging section of the roof. Seen?"

"Seen, Warrant."

"Out-fucking-standing! You have the vision of a goddamned eagle, Troop. Now, do me a favour. Scan that sector and tell me what you see."

I began to do as he had asked, and as I did, I became a little more nervous. I could not see anything that shouldn't be there, except maybe a wasps' nest tucked in the corner. It looked like it had been there a while, but that was about it. I continued to scan intently along the area where the roof met the wall and nothing was obvious, nothing except that nest and some rust.

"Heneghan, what do you see?"

"Warrant, I see . . ."

"Damn it, Troop, speak up! Don't be rude. Don't you know you're wearing a mask that makes it hard for an old guy like me to hear you?"

"Warrant, all I see is a wasps' nest and maybe some rust, Warrant."

"Right! You see that fucking wasps' nest, those sneaky buzzing cunts. Heneghan, does the use of the word *cunt* offend you or in any way feel like harassment toward you?"

"No, Warrant."

"Good. Moving on. Heneghan, the enemy has attached themselves to our unit. This will not do. This is something I will not have at my building. Heneghan, I brought you out here today because I knew you were the man for the job. When I thought to myself, *Who in the hell can take care of a wasp invasion?* I wasted no time in coming up with your name. Do you know why?"

Slightly baffled by what I was hearing, I responded strongly so as to allow my voice to carry, "No, Warrant!"

"Well, two reasons, really: It was near the top of my list this morning, and when the sergeant confirmed you were in the building and otherwise untasked, I thought, *Perfect! Heneghan's our guy.* And make no mistake, Troop, you are our guy . . . mainly because I don't want to do it, and hell, you're already dressed for the occasion. Works out, right?"

"Yeah. How fortunate."

"Well, I'll leave you to it then."

The warrant started to retreat toward the building. Sopping wet from sweat and clouded by confusion, I continued to stand there not knowing what to do.

"Warrant, uh . . . what do you want me to do? I mean, I don't know what to do."

"Hmm. You do bring up a decent tactical issue, Heneghan. With situational awareness like that, you'll be a master private any fucking day now."

After a slight pause and what seemed like an indifferent scan of the area, the warrant walked over to the side door and returned with an old, splintered wooden broom. He held it in his right hand and, with furrowed brow, examined it quickly.

"Yep, that ought to do nicely."

He handed me the dilapidated broom. "Christ, Heneghan, you look like a fucking gladiator. A warrior. You look like a killer. I mean you look ready and willing to wage war. Although, you look like you could use a drink; you're quite overdressed for this kind of weather, Heneghan. Oh, well, no point dwelling on all that. You look ready, my boy."

"Ready for what, Warrant?"

"To get it done. To unleash hell. To wage war on those godless insects of perdition. Oh, also, don't leave any of them little cocksuckers around. I hate wasps. I'm not allergic or anything, but when I'm out here smoking and one of those little yellow cunts starts buzzin' around me, makes me start prancing like Tammy on Toonie Tuesdays at Rusty's Gentleman's . . . never mind . . . just kill 'em all."

With that, the warrant went inside and left me to do his bidding. I waged that battle. And by battle, I mean I swatted awkwardly at the stubborn wasps' nest while encumbered by the oversized gear I was wearing. I swatted and poked at the nest with that rickety old broom until I knocked it loose and it fell to the ground.

Now filled with a blood rage, I proceeded to slam the nest out of existence. I won't lie. I engaged them as if they really were the enemy, blaming them for my discomfort.

When all was said and done, the warrant paraded me in front of everyone and explained how my heroic actions had left PRETC just a little safer, and tonight (being a Friday) I was to be taken care of as I was in need of some cold beer. He also went on to tell any soldier who was willing to listen to get me something to eat. He said I looked sickly, which of course elicited quite the roar of laughter from my fellow brothers- and sisters-in-arms.

I did drink that night. I likely drank my weight in beer. I drank and rattled off the story of the day to any and all who would listen. It, too, elicited quite the roar of laughter on a Friday night. I've never looked at a wasps' nest the same way again. They are my sworn enemy.

# CHAPTER 7

# Escaping Fire

I WALK HOME BENEATH THE black of night. I am sober and consequently deep in thought. I traipse along the paved but cracked sidewalk, almost home. As I ascend the stairs of the fire escape, I am taken aback by an unfamiliar sight on my landing. It is a man—a dishevelled and unkempt man who emits a rather unpleasant odour. He rests there like he is sleeping in his own bed. It is, I suppose—for tonight, anyway.

I open my mouth to speak, to find out what is going on. However, his senses have already alerted him to my presence. He jerks, startled. I raise my hands in a non-threatening way to somehow inform him without words that I am not here to do him any harm. I can tell that he immediately realizes I am innocuous.

"Hey, buddy. I live here," I say, pointing toward the paint-chipped door. I need to get past him to get into my apartment.

He apologetically shifts himself over to allow me a pathway. As I walk by, I hear the sheepish word, "Sorry."

I enter my home, close my front door, and allow myself to rest my back against it. This is the icing on the cake of a very hard week. Earlier in the evening, I had attended a film screening event and was triggered. A few days ago, I was refused another apartment I had applied for. No reason was given, although I suspect being on disability may not have helped. This was the third apartment I had been denied while searching for a more permanent place to call home.

There is another construction project going on downstairs in my current apartment, so I am often awoken by the tremendous sound of a hammer's thud as it nails whatever into whichever, sometimes causing flashbacks. I can think of much better ways to be woken up other than being thrust into torment.

So here I stand behind the door of an apartment that consists of crumbling walls, paper-thin floors, and hammering for an alarm clock, thinking about the movie that held some aggressive triggers and a homeless man who just startled me, sleeping in my stairwell—a perfect cocktail for a depression martini. Straight up. No olive. Tastes like shit.

This is a far cry from where I once was and from who I used to be.

I used to own a home. It had curtains and framed photos of two smiling lovers, hand-picked appliances, a dog, cats, cars—the whole charade. And a charade it was.

I used to wear a uniform. I never had to ask if my job meant something. What I had was pride. Honour. A sense of duty and a drive to fulfill it. Now? Well, now there's an unexpected drunk roommate sleeping outside my door, no more pictures of lovers on my walls, the complete absence of animals, and no fancy vehicles in sight. Just crooked floorboards and poorly fastened cabinet doors, and ghosts who walk behind me, no matter where I go. A far cry from who I once was, indeed.

My initial thought is to go back outside and ask the man to seek refuge somewhere else. But as quickly as that knee-jerk reaction comes to me, it vanishes. It is replaced with a story I start to tell myself about this man on my fire-escape landing: *What if he is a vet? What if he used to be a medic, and this is where life has taken him?* It is in this thought, fact or fable, that a renewed sense of empathy emerges. I open my door and look at this sad, weathered man at my feet.

"Are you warm enough?" I query, knowing the answer cannot possibly be yes.

He responds through a broken series of shameful stutters of "yes." I choose not to believe him. Instead, I go back inside and begin going through my closet for things I no longer wear. I place what I can find into a garbage bag and head outside. Just as I am about to open the door, I see my winter coat hanging on the back of my door. *I can always buy a new one*, I tell myself.

I hand the man the bag and my coat, explaining this is all I can do at this moment. He seems grateful in a humble way, or a drunk way, doesn't matter. I don't need the stuff. He does, sober or otherwise.

I go back inside and sit down on my couch. The cushions envelop me in a cocoon of further depression as I fall victim to its familiar embrace. A car with a very loud muffler rumbles past my apartment, startling me. It reminds me of an incident that occurred sometime in the midway point of 2004.

~

I FOUND MYSELF PRONE ATOP an unkempt hill in the middle of nowhere. I was weighted by my FFO (full fighting order), overlooking a flattened patch of grassland littered with trailers and makeshift huts. Living within that assorted mess of metal and wood was the enemy. Well, kind of. This was all just training, but we were to act as though it really was the enemy. So much so, we had been on our bellies, staring down upon the gaggle of OpFor (opposition forces) for several hours now. Lying on top of the craggy metal of a fully loaded magazine is about as uncomfortable and unpleasant as it gets.

We had arrived when the sun was still visible in the sky. We were to wait for the camouflage of night to engulf the landscape before making our descent into the makeshift village. Beside me, another soldier lay uncomfortable and entangled in the mess of metal, fabric, and plastic that made up our gear. His name was Goss, or as we had affectionately named him, "Goose."

Goose was a funny kid. Christ, we were all kids back then. Goose had been with me since basic training. I had the privilege and, at times, the incredulous horror of watching him get yelled at mercilessly for forgetting his gym socks for PT, or arriving late to formation, and even for wandering the halls of the barracks while wearing his pristine Nike Air Jordans instead of the standard-issue footwear. Goose didn't care much for the rules. Not in a rebellious way, more so in an oblivious sort of manner. Some guys just don't get it. Nonetheless, he passed his basic training course and was now with me at PRETC, a holding platoon in southern Ontario where soldiers would be kept until the start of their trades course. Goose and I had been there for a few months now. My course was not set to start for another several weeks or so, and Goose, well, Goose had been held back a few times for corrective purposes. Basically, he was in shit for sleeping in and missing room inspections, so the army felt that some reinforced training days were needed.

And now here I was on top of a dew-covered hill in the middle of a muggy summer's night right beside Goose. We were in a formation known as all-around defence—essentially on our bellies, weapons pointed out in the shape of a circle, each of us with an arc of fire to observe, allowing for 360 degrees of defence when waiting for a potential enemy.

The sun had been up when we arrived yet was now securely tucked away on the other side of the world. I don't know exactly how long we had been there, but it felt like too long.

And Goose seemed to agree with me, as he kept nodding off and almost losing grip of his weapon, which would be a very bad thing. I had placed my right leg and foot on top of Goose's left leg, and each time I felt him nod off, I would tug my foot toward me sharply, giving him a sudden jolt to encourage him to stay awake. It worked . . . for a while.

At one point during one of Goose's micro-slumbers, he had become so relaxed that he must have unwittingly released the tension of his stomach muscles, because as we all lay in absolute silence and anticipation of further orders, Goose let loose an uproarious and rather lengthy fart. I mean, this fucker scared birds from trees and critters from hiding holes.

Goose was now awake and staring straight ahead with his full concentration. As a hushed snicker of laughter made its way around the circle, Goose leaned in to whisper something in my ear. "Psst, Henny . . . didja hear that fart? Was it loud?"

I really had no idea what to say, and anything I did say was sure to come out steeped in laughter. I was able to compose myself long enough to reply. "Goose, that fart was so fuckin' loud that I'm still waiting for the echo."

Slight laughter arose.

"Shit, really?"

"Dude. It sounded like an arty sim went off in your asshole."

Something took over Goose when he was trying to hold back laughter in a place where it was supremely inappropriate, like a funeral or during a wedding—he clenched his face and allowed his neck to swallow his chin in hopes no sound would come out. He attempted this technique, but it didn't work. Instead, his nose exploded with a projectile snort. And as his nose and mouth betrayed him, the fucker let loose another ass clapper. Now, our all-around defence had transformed into a rabble of cackling hyenas.

This did not please the sergeant. Not one bit. He wandered over toward Goose and me. All I could see when peering out over my rifle sights were two firmly planted feet. My gaze ascended upward until I saw the angry expression of the overlooking sergeant. He bent at the knees, lowering his massive frame to get proximal to the two of us.

He spoke with an urgent yet muted tone: "Which one of you privates is suffering from an inopportune Crohn's outbreak?"

Goose and I remained still and non-verbal in hopes that this was a rhetorical query.

"So you can shit but you can't talk, huh?" He leaned in closer, close enough for me to know he had just finished a cigarette not long before his arrival to our position. "Which one of you is compromising the integrity of this all-around defence with your ill-timed flatulence? I am expecting an answer, Privates."

I sent a sideways glance over to Goose in hopes he would say something. It must have worked because he did. "Uh, Serge, that . . . uh, that was me. I . . . uh, I farted, a bit."

"A bit? A BIT?! Private, you farted so loudly, Osama Bin Hidin' just packed up and moved locations because he thought the Americans had zeroed in and were dropping bombs on his mountainside!

Laughter erupted throughout the ranks. This of course was quickly silenced when the troops could feel the roving gaze of the vexed sergeant scanning over each of us.

"Private Goose, I am not a doctor, nor am I, like Henny here, a medic. What I *am* is a sergeant telling you that should you let another sound escape that unfortunately loose rectum of yours, I will firmly cement my boot up your ass so far that should I wiggle my toes, the roof of your mouth will start to tickle, understood?"

"Yes, Sergeant."

"Good. As for the rest of you, you smell like shit. Prepare to move."

Goose looked at me and I at him. We masked our laughter.

We were given the order to make our way down toward the village. The mock scenario was that the village had been overrun by the Taliban, and we were to engage with and eliminate the hostiles. The tips of our weapons were fit with BFAs (blank firing attachments). These were used when shooting blank rounds, to simulate real bullets and thus real magazine changes.

The clatter of battle began.

*Pop, pop-pop, pop . . . pop-pop-pop, pop-pop!*

Goose and I had made our way under a detached semi-trailer and once again got into the prone position. This seemed as advantageous a position as any. Goose and I started firing arbitrarily at the enemy while performing skilled magazine changes upon emptying the ones in our respective rifles.

"Firing! Covering! Reloading!" was the song sung back and forth between us as we continued to partake in this virtual bloodbath.

At some point, two non-combatants had joined us beneath the trailer—two females who were playing the parts of villagers. I was in the middle of a magazine change when Goose halted me and said through an overly enthusiastic smirk, "Henny, I have this!"

He slowly reached down to his side and withdrew a T-flash (a pyrotechnic designed to simulate a grenade). His smirk had now grown into an evil ear-to-ear smile.

"Should I throw it?"

"Well, I doubt you're supposed to get close to it, name it, and love it. Yeah, throw the fuckin' thing!"

In retrospect, I should have told him to hold, name, and love it.

Goose removed the cap and struck it against itself to ignite the charge. He then became mesmerized by the glowing embers of the now lit and live ordnance.

"Goose. GOOSE!"

"Huh, yeah?"

"Throw the fucking thing."

"Oh, shit . . . yeah."

Goose reared his arm back and flung it, arm up and outward, releasing the flaming stick of death. Sadly, he did not take into account the fact that the trailer we were seeking cover beneath was overhead, and as such, the T-flash hit said trailer and fell ominously to the grass right in front of us. It rolled about a foot and a half away from our faces.

Like a scene from a movie, Goose shot a glance at me—and me to him. We both looked back toward the nearby T-flash rocking back and forth on the spot. The two female villagers had seen this grievous toss and now shared our concern for our unfortunate circumstance. And in one harmonious sync of our voices we exclaimed, "Oh . . . fuck . . ."

And with that, we tucked our heads and hoped for the best.

The blast went off, and the sudden rush of violent air blew inward, outward, and upward. I felt it against my hands and clothing. A deafening ring played in my ears, and when I opened my eyes to take inventory of myself to ensure that all was okay, I was met with Goose's big dumb face smiling back at me.

I have never wanted to punch a friend more in my life.

The battle would end, and all would be okay. The two villagers were also forgiving of the incident, one of them even gifting a new nickname to Goose: Pillow Hands. "Nice toss, Pillow Hands."

It was almost five in the morning by the time we had gathered our gear and picked up the spent brass. I had even picked up a piece of the T-flash and kept it as a keepsake of the near miss. I'm not sure where it is now, though. The group of tired troops all gathered into the back of the troop-carrying vehicle and readied to head back to the barracks.

The back of a military land vehicle is a loud and cantankerous ride. Amidst the sharp ringing assaulting my inner ears and the cacophonous rattling of the transportation, a new sound emerged—a clearly audible and thunderous fart.

"GOOSE!"

"Sorry, Sergeant."

# CHAPTER 8

# Falls

I AWAKE TO THE SOUND of hammers striking walls: *Thud. Thud. Thud!* Despite the depressing interruption to my sleep, I persuade myself to get out of bed and go have a shower.

After I shower, I watch the minutes turn into hours as time passes on the clock. Neglecting to eat, I suddenly realize I am supposed to go to therapy. One would think therapy on a day like this would be a good thing. I'm not sure. I cancel last minute. This action is not rooted in any discontent toward my therapist. It is more the fact I feel too angry to even converse. Too irritated to even articulate. And I think I am coming down with a man-cold.

I sit in my apartment, pondering the life I used to have and the one I currently live. The differences between the two are stark and numbing. I feel like I am in a boxing ring, fighting remembrance. My mind bleeds, taking a pounding.

In a fit of quiet and internalized rage, I pack a bag. I then release that quiet anger, screaming down to the hammer-wielding menace downstairs. I punch the floor to accent my point, call a hotel in Niagara, and take off. I run away. I am fully aware I cannot outrun these issues—my unseen but very real opponents—but, goddammit, I want to, and I will try. I am falling, getting knocked down. Gravity. I remember a different kind of fall, a more literal fall when I was still in training in Ontario.

~

WE'VE ALL BEEN HIT BY those late-night cravings at some time or another in our lives. And generally, late at night, there is rarely a healthy selection to choose from. We've all fallen victim to some semblance of a fast-food joint, I am sure.

When I was still fairly new to the army, I rarely bucked routine. I was compliant. This included meal times. Monday: chicken. Tuesday: roast (burnt, but roast). Wednesday: steak (neither rare nor well done—shoe leather, more like). Thursday: veal or some mystery meat. Each day of each week was the same culinary delectation served over and over again for months on end. Don't get me wrong, the food wasn't bad. Not really, anyway. It just lacked creativity and selection. As such, the occasional venture from base to the local sandwich shop or rusted-down diner wasn't out of the ordinary for soldiers who had their civilian vehicles with them. Since I was not one such soldier, I was usually at the mercy of our army cooks and their chosen menus.

However, weekends were a different story. Many soldiers would cab it into the next closest city to enjoy the nightlife and the ample pub fare. This often meant sharing the cost of the taxi rather than spending your hard-earned private's salary on a solo trip, making leaving base more feasible.

One such weekend, some friends and I went out for a night of pure debauchery, bouncing from pub to pub and club to club until our ringing ears finally had enough. It was time to go home. We walked in an exaggerated serpentine pattern; the sidewalk felt like it was narrowing. Alex had called a cab so we were all on the lookout. Sadly, in our state, we thought every passing pair of headlights was our arriving taxi.

A typical response would be: "Hey! That'tss the scab . . . Never mind . . . it's snot it." *Hiccup.*

The cab would eventually find us, of course. I suppose it's not hard to find a gaggle of relatively fit, shaven-head rapscallions standing on a street corner. Bless those taxi drivers, putting up with our obnoxious, loud, and slurred conversations while driving us home to the base every weekend.

On our way back that night, someone had broken through the noise of competing voices and made mention of getting some food. *Great idea.* Alex was up front with our godsend of a taxi driver and requested a stop at a burger joint just outside of the base. The cabbie was happy to oblige. He was about to sit in a drive-thru while six drunken soldiers made food orders—more bank for him, and it was.

I made my request known come my turn. "Hi, ma'am, um, I'll get the schicken sammich, and a Coke, please."

"You want large fries or regular?"

"Let's . . . better go with . . . uh, large, thanks!"

"Okay, please pull forward to the next window."

Alex handed us our chosen trans-fat bounties on the ride back to base. I didn't touch mine until the driver had stopped and we got out. I decided I would wait until I was back in my shared room before diving into anything. That was the plan, anyway. It didn't turn out that way. My young, starving stomach sent word from below that I was to tear into the brown paper bag and retrieve the stupendous poultry delight—and inhale it savagely. Not being one to argue with my stomach too often, I reached in and withdrew the chicken burger and peeled back the lid of its box before I lifted it to take a gigantic and uncoordinated bite. I felt the mayo from inside the bun stick to the corners of my mouth and slink outward to the sides of my cheeks. Bits of shredded lettuce dangled on my chin before falling helplessly to the waxy floor below.

I arrived on my floor and yanked back the door leading into the hallway. *I am almost home—eat this and pass out,* I thought. Unfortunately, the universe had other ideas in mind for me. I looked up from my ever-shrinking burger to see someone standing outside my room. It was a woman. She was conversing with one of my roommates. As I got closer, I received confirmation that the woman was Johansson. She was also training to be a medic, as competitive as she was stunning. Johansson kept up with her male counterparts during the most vigorous of physical training sessions by way of her sheer iron will. She was tough. This made her even more captivating. And there she was, standing by *my* door. On any other occasion, this would have been a moment scripted from fantasy. But currently, I was as drunk as a midnight sailor on furlough, adorned with fallen lettuce and sticky mayonnaise. Not a good look.

I had already sauntered too far down the hall to be able to turn and go back; however, the thought had come to mind. But before I knew it, both she and my roommate turned their respective heads and looked straight at me.

"Hey, Henny," Garon said. "Just getting back, eh? How was it?"

Currently churning a mouthful of synthetic chicken, I was unable to respond right away, though I tried through a series of disjointed head nods.

"That good, huh? Atta boy."

"Henny, how are ya?" Johansson chimed in.

Finally able to swallow and respond, I informed them both that I was good and the night was a success, as made evident by the half-eaten chicken burger in my hand.

"Chicken burger. Good call, Henny!" Her voice sounded like music, even if it was competing against the fog that had rolled into my head.

Having exchanged greetings, I expected Garon and Johansson to move and allow access to my room so I could sneak in and hide my hideousness from them. Nope. He did not move. Nor did she. Instead, they simply returned to their conversation, occasionally throwing a glance toward me to make me feel included. This was bad. It was bad because I was still ravenously hungry, yet I have a thing where I cannot eat in front of people who are not eating. So I stood there with sloppy chicken in hand, just waiting. Waiting and offering smirks when looked at. It was also bad because this gave my drunk soldier's brain time for introspection. And this was not good because as drunk as I was, I really couldn't afford to concentrate on numerous things at once such as holding a conversation and hanging onto food at the same time. My hand slackened its grip on the chicken burger.

It loosed to the point where mayo took over and offered the *poulet* a method of escape—sliding out of the bun. And slide it did. The next sequence of events has since transformed into slow-motion memories for me. *Thanks, brain.* The breaded delight began a methodical free fall, causing a swooshing sound as it flipped and twirled along its descent. I swear, we three had time to watch it fall and remark at the same time, "Chicken down!"

It landed with a splatter and smack on the hallway floor at my feet. All I could do was gawk at it. And that's precisely what I did, until a soothing voice commanded my attention.

"Oh, no, Henny, your burger. Chicken down."

I responded with what I had hoped was a casual and suitable retort. "Yeah, nah, it'ss sfine! I was done anyway."

Garon countered, "But you have half a bun and shit left."

"Yeah . . . I'm . . . I got full. Full."

"Well, that's fine then, right?" Johansson assured. She and Garon then re-engaged in conversation, with the occasional glance thrown at the now pathetic chicken patty lying at my toes. Fearing that Johansson would have thought me a cretin if I bent down to pick this up (yes, this is drunk brain at work) and knowing I could not rightly leave it where it lay, I instead decided to use my heel in a backward shovelling motion to remove said downed chicken from sight. I extended one foot and attempted to sneakily slide the chicken to the rear of my person to shield poor Johansson's eyes from it.

Surprisingly, it worked. Neither of them saw a thing. *Success!* However, they were rather intently engrossed in conversation with one another. This meant Garon was still not moving from the doorway and I was still stranded beside a beautiful woman, all the while looking repugnant. And yes, it meant further introspection, plotting, and planning from drunk brain.

Drunk brain sent word from above that I was still hungry. I reminded drunk brain that we had experienced a culinary casualty and we were now left wanting. Drunk brain gave coordinates to my eyes and forced them to look at my hand—there, in my hand, were the surviving remnants of Corporal Chicken Burger: bun, mayo, and lettuce.

*Eat it!*

*No, she's standing right there.*

*Eat it!*

*Brain, you know I can't.*

*EAT IT, GODDAMNIT!*

And with that, drunk brain commanded I lift the now soggy sesame seed bun toward my mouth. I obliged, helplessly so. He was right—we might die; we were so hungry! Without hesitation, I opened my mouth and guided the disintegrating bun and its dripping mayo toward my cavernous face hole. With an unsteady hand, I bounced it off my bottom lip and chin, then upper lip and the tip of my nose before successfully biting down into the gelatinous bun and its seeds. No matter, the mission was a success. I now had food headed for the starved village of stomach.

I noticed a deafening silence sweep through the halls. I looked up to investigate. To my horror (and hers), both Johansson and Garon had ceased talking to one another and had witnessed the entire encounter.

"Bro, did you just eat mayo, bun, and lettuce?"

I needed to deny this at once. So I opened my mouth and tried to rebuke Garon's claim. Regrettably, as I did, not only was my response suffocated in a wallowing vat of saliva, mayo, lettuce, and bun, but the vehemence with which I had attempted to speak my denial caused a sudden ejection of said saliva, mayo, lettuce, and bun—a projectile that left my mouth with the force of a bullet from a gun and landed on Johansson's chin.

I watched as she winced and jerked at the sudden slap of chewed food to her face. I was mortified. There was a brief unspoken void between all of us. Garon broke it with a belt of laughter as he doubled over, finally moving from the fucking doorway.

I knew I had to apologize, and I really wanted to. But the thing was, as is the case anytime you consume fast food, I now had to use the bathroom—immediately. So I began bolting past Garon and Johansson while orating my apology as I penguin-stepped by the laughing duo.

I slammed the door to the bathroom and remained there until I was sure Johansson had left.

Come morning, I was still in the bathroom. Johansson hadn't spent the night or anything, I had just passed out, was all. I woke to a booming headache and cotton mouth. I slunk from the bathroom and was greeted by the sight of sleeping roommates. I slid out into the hallway. I was going to find a water fountain and cure the first part of my self-induced ailments.

I closed the door quietly behind me and turned to head down the hall. Before I could take another step, I froze in place. Resting there before me was a reminder of the horrific incidents of last night's debacle—a pathetic looking, half-ingested, mayo-lathered chicken patty.

Chicken down!

~

NOW, TODAY, IT IS MAN down instead. I make it to Niagara Falls and check into a hotel and shut the blinds. No more outside world. I have a Jacuzzi in my room, so that's the first place I go. I melt into the warm bubbles of expensive comfort for the afternoon. At least there is no hammering. Worth the price.

On day two, the man-cold reaches its full potential. I stay in bed all day, managing to catch some uninterrupted sleep for the first time in a very long time.

On day three, I am shaken to semi-consciousness by an utterly awful nightmare, confronted by a dark room. Nothing around me is familiar. *Where am I? What is going on?* I am already in a heightened state of terror from the dream. I panic, swimming through a sea of blankets until I find my way to the floor. Things aren't improving. The floor feels nothing like the one in my apartment. I can barely catch my breath. I am consumed with fear. Slowly my eyes catch sight of a light sneaking its way in from underneath the door. I scramble over to it and begin climbing up the door frame with my clammy hands. After fumbling with the locking mechanism, I pull the door open and find myself looking into an empty hallway, hearing the sounds of a buzzing vending machine. My panting breaths of fear and confusion slow. I remember where I am now. I start to come back.

I go inside my room and allow the door to close under its own power. I crumple to the floor and sit on my knees in a pitiful display of personal defeat. I feel like a child, alone and scared. In this moment, all I want is someone to wrap their arms around me and comfort me, whispering it's going to be all right. That everything is going to be okay. But that is a fantasy. I am alone. Horribly alone. Only the ghosts of my dreams linger and sit with me.

In this moment, depression and PTSD feel a lot like gravity. It is a force sitting on my shoulders, insisting I look down, demanding I stagger and fall. Depression feels like you're not alive, you're just awake. Always awake, tirelessly aware of just how different you are from the rest of the world.

# CHAPTER 9

## Silence

I AM IN MY APARTMENT at night, and my phone sits beside me on the couch. It lights up: MUM CELL. I pick it up and press the green ANSWER button and hold the small speaker to my ear. On the other end a subtle metallic tone breaks through, followed by a greeting: "Matthew . . ."

I immediately know something is wrong by the way she speaks. Her voice is shaking and shrouded in a noticeable sadness. I begin to talk empathetically, responding to her. Almost instinctively, my medic brain switches on, and my mum becomes my patient.

Skillfully, I begin to pry answers from her in an attempt to unearth the true nature of her suffering. She explains, "I am ill."

This is nothing new. My mother has been sick for most of my life. But what is out of character is she claims her living conditions are rapidly becoming equal to squalor.

Although I can't get her to elaborate about what she means by "very ill," I know she has battled mental illnesses for as long as I have been alive, so I surmise a meaning.

Our conversation quickly grows a little more serious when she begins to explain she wants to die and how she plans to make this happen. My heart rate involuntarily quickens with concern. I rely on my medic skills, coupled with being a very worried son, to figure out what she is planning.

In the past, and when I was too young to really comprehend, my mother did try to kill herself. She swallowed a perfect combination of pills to warrant emergency intervention. I didn't know it at the time, but I almost lost my mother after already losing my father. My brothers and sisters were burdened with not only being older and bearing witness to this event, but with having to look after me—a confused, clueless young boy. Well, that's not the case anymore: I am anything but clueless. Confused? Perhaps.

I feel the conversation drawing to a close at my mother's choosing. She ends the discussion with, "I love you Matt, okay? No matter what, Mum loves you."

*Click.*

The line goes dead.

I pause for a split second as I place the phone back down beside me. *What would I do as a medic in this situation?* I immediately call the police. My mother lives across the country, so a quick jaunt over to check in with her is out of the question.

I speak to a kind dispatcher who concurs that my concerns seem legitimate. She dispatches a young RCMP officer to my mother's residence to check in on her. Tonight, I need my mum just like I needed her in August 2006.

~

I was awake and lying on my bunk within the barracks. As I lay on my back, I draped one arm lazily over my face in an attempt to block out the vexing ambient light of the street lamp outside. The standard-issue curtains did little to stop its intrusive orange glimmer. I also had one foot securely planted on the floor while the rest of me was splayed on top of the paper-thin army mattress.

Why? The room was spinning with a merciless rotation, and the thick heat from the summer's night air was not helping. I was drunk. Very, very drunk. We all were.

On a black August night, a slew of intoxicated soldiers were strewn from end to end in temporary living quarters. We were slated to stay there for a night or two. Earlier in the evening, the halls had been reverberating with an eclectic mix of Jimi Hendrix, AC/DC, and a very out of place Backstreet Boys. There was no one set DJ for this hallway shindig—whoever had the loudest speakers seemed to dictate the choice of song. There was an endless array of alcoholic beverages to choose from. Beer, whisky, something fruity, you name it, it was there somewhere. Each room brought about a new and unique partying experience. No matter which room you wandered into, it was bound to be filled with boisterous laughter and an unsanctioned cigarette being frantically inhaled by a person sitting on a windowsill beside an open window. Occasionally they would blow smoke sideways from a crooked corner of their mouth before chiming in with either the chorus of whatever song was currently playing or doling out what they thought to be life wisdom to a limited and fleetingly interested audience. It was a party—at least, it appeared that way.

Within each room, there were stark reminders of what was to come the following day. Crisp military-green dress uniforms were either hung in garment bags or carefully placed on a hanger attached to the bathroom shower rod. Although we hid behind a veil of cheerful and somewhat juvenile (bordering on delinquent) behaviour, we all knew the reality of what tomorrow would bring. We had already been given an unforgettable reminder of what that was earlier in the day, long before the festivities had started. These "festivities" were nothing more than a way to drown sadness and the sombre ideations that accompanied it. We were drinking to forget. Some of us drank to obliteration. Others, like myself, consumed one too many until the world started to spin. We drank with a purpose.

Earlier in the day, we had the honourable but sorrowful task of retrieving one of our fallen brothers off a plane recently returned from Afghanistan. War had claimed his life, and all that was sent back to us and his home were the remains of a hero and the unmitigated reminders of what soldiers experienced over there. There is nothing I have faced or can fathom to face in this life more heartbreaking than holding the cold steel of a flag-draped casket, knowing one of your own is inside. It is ironic that it is completely and undeniably sobering, and yet it forces you to lust for anything but sobriety.

After the "party," I was confronted with a spinning room and the ferocious battle to keep whatever I had eaten securely stowed within my now churning stomach—a war in its own right, and one I was slowly losing. Eventually a heavy saliva introduced itself to my mouth and informed me I had lost the battle. At any moment, I was going to be re-acquainted with my culinary choices of the day. I struggled but succeeded to fight the crippling gravity that held me to my bed and rose to my feet. After a couple of failed attempts at forward momentum, I pushed ahead with one foot, then the other. My heavily intoxicated gait was likely equal to walking the halls of a rocking ship, punished by the relentless stormy sea. After bouncing from wall to wall down the corridor, I found myself in the welcoming embrace of a brightly lit military bathroom. The open stall almost called for me, and as I continued to stumble, I made my way closer to the throne. I had no problem kneeling before this one, and kneel I did.

I crumpled to my knees inside the stall and closed the door behind me. I proceeded to violently but accurately vomit all my bad decisions into the toilet. The sober me started thinking, *Well, guess you won't be doing that again, eh, big guy!* At the same time, my pizza, nachos, nine beers, three shots, and one old fashioned hurled forth in a haste. When all was said and done, I leaned against the cold metal walls of the stall, allowing their comforting chill to permeate my clammy skin. With failed coordination, I reached for some tissue paper to clean the evidence away from my chin. I likely resembled a baby reaching out for a mobile hanging above them.

As I waited for my stomach to give me the all clear to return to bed, I heard the shuffling but panicked steps of someone else having also entered the bathroom. He barrelled toward another open stall with a cacophony mimicking what I had just done moments ago. I remember smiling to myself for an instant because I knew exactly who it was. When you live so close to others in those types of living conditions for as long as soldiers do, you can identify someone just by the way they breathe. I was relieved in knowing I was not the only one fighting a losing battle with Jameson.

I listened without really wanting to as my squad mate grunted and groaned his way through a series of agonizing wretches. When the battle seemed to have quieted, I slurred a genuine "You okay, bud?" An answer was returned in the form of a chuckle and what I presumed to be a thumbs-up, which I could not see through the three or four metal stall walls that separated us. I knew he was fine—as fine as any of us could be, anyway.

After a few moments spent in heavy breathing, and from those few stalls down, my brother spoke a simple phrase aloud, chilling me into sobriety. The words he said were "Sucks, ya know? It just . . . sucks . . ."

He was right. It did suck, and he was not referring to the level of our inebriation. He was talking about something much more meaningful. He was referring to the fact that, in a few short hours and over the next several days from this moment we were having in the bathroom, we were going to have to once again clasp our hands around the cold steel of an enclosed metal box and carry the remains of a fallen comrade from hearse to plane, from plane to hearse, and from hearse to grave. That volley of thoughts was about as reverberant as it gets.

It's funny, the silence we shared from the moment my friend stated the obvious to the moment I was able to leave the bathroom was the time we "said" the most to one another. Our silence spoke volumes. To this day, I think it is one of the more meaningful conversations I have ever had.

When I was satisfied in knowing the vomiting was over, I cracked a joke with my now sleeping squaddie and returned to my room. I lay on my rack and attempted to get comfortable—a task not always easy when deep in thought and intoxication.

Beside me lay my cellphone. I looked at it for a moment with a childlike yearning. I wanted to call my mum. I wanted to tell her what I was going to have to do in the coming days. I wanted to explain to her that, after carrying the casket of a fallen brother earlier in the day, I had also spent six long hours in an aircraft hangar, learning how to remove, hold, and then fold our nation's flag so that it could be given to a grieving family. She used to love the TV show *Tour of Duty*, and I recalled thinking back to an episode we had watched together, an episode reminiscent of the current situation. I wanted to call her and cry while telling her how heavy and real this all was. How it was nothing like what we had seen on TV. I wanted to, but I couldn't. She wasn't speaking with me—a day or so prior, we had gotten into an argument. Calling Mum wasn't an option, but I tried anyway. No answer. Silence can be sobering, too.

Corporal Andrew James Eykelenboom, or Boomer as we called him, a medic, aged twenty-three, gave his life in service to his country, to you, to me, to all of us. A few days after his death, I stood alongside my remaining brothers on a runway after having just placed a flag-draped casket into the mouth of an awaiting hearse.

The next day I stood in a row of four. Across from me, another row of four. We stared at one another and did not move, statues of discipline. When I caught sight of Boomer's mother and father, I remained still. They slowly walked toward the wheeled tomb now encasing their son. We stood on either side of them. Amid the hum of jet engines, I could hear horrible sobs of bereavement leave the chest of Maureen, Boomer's mom. Behind them, a tall figure who resembled the dead man with unmatched accuracy— Boomer's brother. All I could do was watch and do nothing.

On the outside, I was the perfect carving of a soldier, stoic and still. On the inside, I was disintegrating into a wounded boy, a vulnerable child. A child who felt inadequate.

Later that evening after the service, we found ourselves once more shoulder to shoulder—this time sitting at the bar. We each held a cold bottle or glass in hand. The news on the pub TV screamed at us, showing us images of earlier in the day. We watched ourselves in third person, carrying the remains of our fallen brother. What a surreal moment. No amount of training could have prepared me. It was fucking awful.

~

BACK IN MY APARTMENT, I await word about my mum. My phone rings again. I jump. Caller: BLOCKED NUMBER. I pick up immediately, apprehensive and a little panicked. It is the RCMP officer. He explains how he went out to check up on my mother.

"She's a nice old lady," he mentions. "I gotta say, one of the cleanest places I have ever been in."

*What the hell? That isn't what Mum said.*

The RCMP officer satisfies my line of questioning by explaining there was plenty of food in the home, and there were no safety concerns with the accommodations. I exhale. At least she is safe. I am confused but relieved.

The relief is temporary, however. My mum messages me to tell me she is angry because I contacted the police, and she doesn't want to talk to me anymore. The next morning at 6:36 a.m., after a sleepless night plagued by nightmares, I would love nothing more than to speak to her. I am a grown man, yes—but still just a boy when it comes to thinking about Mum. My mother's silence is all too familiar.

CHAPTER 10

# Abort Mission

DEPRESSION BRINGS ME HERE, BUT distraction holds me in place. I am at a bar, not an uncommon backdrop for me. It is a quiet little pub. A guitarist in the corner of the room strums his feelings away on a worn marigold Washburn—each chord a sad tune just for me.

The bartender comes and hands me a glass filled with a rust-coloured panacea. The diversion I ordered—whisky, single malt. I sit alone in the company of a thousand thoughts. I rub the sides of the glass, hoping for the genie of intoxication to grant me the wish of a numbing respite. The ethereal wish granter never appears, but someone else does.

My nose becomes seduced by a wandering perfume: a subtle strawberry and vanilla. I turn my head in search of this delightful scent. There, off to my right, stand two women—friends who are obviously on a night out. They pull some chairs away from the bar and sit down near the end. I return my gaze to an almost depleted glass of whisky. During the last swig, a happy memory materializes and floats into the forefront: Colin, my brother-in-arms.

~

COLIN WILMOT AND I WERE both medics at CFRB Edmonton, training for deployment to Afghanistan. "Henny, your gym shoes smell like . . . gym shoes!" Wilmot impishly grimaced.

"Yeah, sorry, dude . . . what can I say? Blame the army." We both snickered as he continued to help me stretch. Our unit had just returned from morning PT. On this day, it had been a marathon-style run around the base. Our commanding officer was a former Skyhawk (member of the ceremonial parachute company), so he expected high standards of physical fitness. As such, we were run into the ground. And on a hot summer morning, too.

Colin, or Wilmot as he was more commonly called, had the unfortunate task of helping me stretch after said run. This included a hamstring stretch that would see my foot in close proximity to his face—much to his dismay.

"So, other than try to kill me by way of foot rot, what do we have going on tonight?" Colin was asking because earlier in the week we had made plans for him to spend the night at my place and head out for a couple of wobbly pops. He was going through some relationship stuff and so was I. I confided in Colin a lot; he was easy to talk to. He was a young man with an old soul, a soul with many years of lived experience beyond the diminutive number of his age.

"Oh, you know, have a couple at my place, get ready, and head out to the pub. Chat with the ladies, no?"

"Sure, Henny. It's your operation. Lead the way."

We finished out the day's training, which included cleaning and counting inventory as well as weapons. As the day neared its end, the clock seemed to slow down. We were sitting in formation, waiting for dismissal for the weekend. There was an itch of excitement shared by Colin and me. We were ready to get this party started. Colin always knew how to crack a good joke, but it was more his permanent smile and somewhat goofy disposition that made being around him such a delight.

I could feel sweat crawl down my neck and join the other slithering rivulets along my back. It had been a scorcher today. Eventually the time came, and the sergeant gave us furlough for the weekend. But not before boisterously demanding "No one is to end up in jail" and "No one better get anyone else pregnant" and finally: "We'd best not beat up any civilians." Standard parting words before a weekend sure to boast nice weather.

Colin and I made our way to my place downtown where we could get together for a weekend of unsupervised tomfoolery. It would also give me added time to pick his brain about some relationship challenges I was having with my girlfriend. He was always kind and good at giving advice. He was skilled in the art of empathy. Colin was a good friend.

Once at my place, it took little time before the discernible hiss of a loosening beer cap was heard.

"Cheers!"

Colin and I sat on the front porch of my humble apartment and watched the traffic of a bustling city glide by. The sun removed its blazing yellow hue and donned its evening best, a brilliantly flawless orange. It began to lower itself in behind the beanstalks of the city's skyline.

"So where we headed, boss?"

"Well, my son, we're goin' flirtin'!"

"Shit! All right, let's go."

Colin was a good-looking kid. Fit and athletic, he boasted a tapestry of ink on his skin. He was a popular guy.

I went into my room and threw on a shirt I felt best fit my physique. My confidence was not exactly soaring these days with all the contentions I was having in my relationship—things I would later discuss with Colin during a drunken nightcap. But now, it was time to get Colin out to have some fun.

We set off on foot to the bar district downtown, playfully jostling with one another as we passed the hordes along the sidewalk. We stared intimidatingly at anyone who made lingering eye contact with one of us that we deemed hostile—even in civilian clothing, we were brothers-in-arms.

We made it to the bar—a trendy downtown spot boasting an appropriate amount of fluorescent lighting and wooden accent. It was a more mature crowd, so this was one of my favourite spots to come for a cold one. Colin found a table by the window where we could people-watch, and I went to the bar to procure the first beverages of the outing. I returned to the table, and after some lighthearted banter, I began poking him for wisdom.

"Bro, do you think it's selfish to go overseas and leave family behind?" Something I was slated to do later that year.

"What? Selfish? Hell no, man. Going overseas is what we do. It's the least selfish thing any person can do in my eyes."

This had been a question saturating my daily thoughts for some time now.

Colin continued: "Dude, you are not selfish. You know why? Because you're doing something the majority of the world will never do—sacrificing yourself, your time, your life if need be, for someone else. A stranger. There's nothing selfish in that. Why do you think I demanded to be put on as an alternate for the tour?"

Colin was newer to the unit. Newer than I was, anyway. As such, he was not scheduled for this deployment. But that didn't stop him from training as though he were going to deploy tomorrow. Come hell or high water, Wilmot was going to Afghanistan—he'd make sure of that. I spoke again: "Thanks, brother. Sorry, don't mean to drag the evening down. It's just been weighing on me is all."

"Troop, don't apologize. Drink!"

"Sir, yes, sir!" And drink we did.

While procuring another round for a now lubricated Colin and me, my eyes caught sight of something of magnificent potential—two gorgeous women sitting together at a table close to ours.

I got the elixir of the night and wandered back over to our seats, but not before giving a sideways glance at the two women, confirming just how striking they were.

"Here ya go, bud. Hey, Wilmot, check my six, then to the right of the support beam. Seen?"

"Seen."

"Good. Now, I'm kind of drunk, so I need you to confirm. The two targets in the area of operation, are they green light or not?"

Colin proceeded to casually glance over my shoulder toward the aforementioned table.

"Target is green. Target is green. Target is *very* green."

This confirmation evoked the need to peer over my own shoulder and take sight of them once more before the following: "Colin, there are two pretty women sitting over there by themselves in an establishment of troglodytes and hippy civilians. We as soldiers cannot allow this to be the case, seen?"

Slight laughter.

"Seen."

"All right, you're second in order of march. I'll approach from their three o'clock and make visuals known. Once I start talking, come around my six and stand at their four o'clock just in behind me. I'll introduce us and request to join 'em, yeah?"

"Fuck, if you say so, man."

And with that, we rolled out. I approached the table and initiated contact with what I hoped was a charming smile and pleasing demeanour. It seemed to have worked as smiles were given back to us. We entered into some idle chit-chat for a few moments, and to my surprise we were asked to join them.

Colin and I sat down and began conversing with the two women. They were witty and intelligent. Laughs were had, stories were shared, and flirtations were abundant. This was a great evening.

"So what do you guys do?" one of the women asked. Filled with a slight bravado and liquid confidence, I leaned most of my weight on one elbow resting atop the table and replied, "Well, Wilmot here is a combat medic, kinda like a doctor, if you will. And I am a little above him in rank, but I'm a medic, too—we're in the army." An arrogant grin had now drawn itself onto my face. The two ladies were speechless. They looked at one another and then back toward Colin and me. Before they could say anything, I said pretentiously, "It's true. We're soldiers." The two women looked at one another quickly once more and then back toward us. What happened next was unforeseeable.

"Oh. My. God. Yes! I knew I recognized you guys. You're with Field Ambulance, right?"

That pompous smirk I had been wearing began to soften slightly. Colin's back stiffened in kind.

"Uh, yeah . . . yeah, we are."

"Oh, too funny. We are nursing officers—we are in the same unit."

Officers? These two beautiful women were officers in *our* unit? *SHIT!*

My eyes widened, and I swallowed my own throat.

"Small world. I have to go to the bathroom, be right back," Colin said as he excused himself sheepishly from the table.

He walked with a gait that, had I not known better, I would have speculated he had soiled himself. So now I was left in the company of two commanding officers whom I had spent the greater part of the night fraternizing with (something highly against policy). I took this as an opportunity to offer to buy drinks and gain some separation so I could plan our egress from the situation. I grabbed the drinks for the women first and dropped them off. When I returned with Wilmot's beer, I noticed he was still not at the table. But that's not all I noticed—as I looked past the officers, I could see the bay window at the end of the bar. Standing outside was Colin. He was motioning to me with a quick and spastic throat-cutting gesture and mouthing the words, "Get out of there. Abort! Abort!"

Knowing I was now a solo man in a dangerous area of operation, I concocted a plan. I was going to reach into my pocket, withdraw my flip phone, and pretend I was receiving an important phone call. I would then excuse myself to find quieter ground so as to complete the fictitious call. I took a sip from my drink and then overenthusiastically reacted to an "incoming" call. I pressed the phone to my ear and motioned to the women that I would return. I, of course, would not return. Colin and I ran back to my place, sporadically stopping to stagger and chuckle at the evening's unfortunate events.

Back at my apartment, Colin and I had a couple more beers and a few more laughs before turning in for the night.

"Hey, Henny—thanks for a great night. I needed it."

"Sure thing. Get some sleep. I'll see ya in the morning."

Colin racked out on the couch, and I passed out, still fully dressed, on top of my bed. Come morning, Colin was gone, and the blankets I had given him were neatly folded and placed on one side of the couch. A note was left behind:

Hey, Henny.

Thanks again for a great time. It was a blast. Can't wait till Monday. See what happens with all this officer stuff . . . I blame you! Haha. Kidding. Have a great weekend, buddy.

Wilmot

# CHAPTER 11

# Veteran

I HEAD OUT TO A clinic that often deals with veterans. I am confronted by a pile of poignant questionnaires. I am told to answer honestly, so I do. I work through the arduous task, and when I circle the answer to the final question, I am left with a lingering sense of feeling broken, weak, and unworthy. Feeling alone. Alone because I *am* alone. Not just in the waiting room but in the general sense of the word. I sit quietly, observing the eggshell-coloured reception room. I remain there, unwittingly taking inventory of my surroundings in such a way that if asked to, I could re-create that room in its entirety, right down to where the three receptionists were seated. I do this until my ears ring with the calling of my name: "Heneghan, Mr. Heneghan . . ."

My body snaps into a tight, rigid frame as I answer back, "Sir. Here, sir."

"Right this way."

"Yes, sir."

I follow behind the statuesque man who had just belted out my name. He walks me through a winding hallway adorned with pictures of the past: Passchendaele, Dieppe, Vimy, Ortona—all greyed-out images with men standing triumphantly at the forefront. Some are smiling, some are merely smirking, and others are just stoically posing for the camera. I feel unworthy in their company. Those men, all those generations ago, had been through so much and yet still had the stout-heartedness to return home and to live normal, happy, and fulfilling lives. Not without their trials and tribulations, I'm sure. Regardless, I am a thirty-four-year-old man, having served only six years in the army, a paid education in health care, who can barely fake my way through a normal day. I would hate to imagine what they would see in a picture of me.

I am shown a seat. The large-framed man, a nurse, begins asking me more questions. And more questions. And then, more questions. All of them have sinister answers.

"Have you ever wanted to harm yourself or others?"

"Yes."

"Have you ever had thoughts of suicide?"

"Yes."

"Do you want to die?"

"Yes."

And on they go. I answer; he writes. I then step on a scale, have my blood pressure checked, and have my height measured. It is all so impersonal. Methodical. When he is satisfied he has collected what he needs from me, he walks me back through the winding hallway, back into the waiting room, and informs me the doctor will be out in a minute to see me. I acknowledge and proceed to wait. Anxiously.

I don't know how much stamina I have left for answering questions about how terrible I feel. To be honest, most days after I shower and wipe the steam away from the mirror, I see an out-of-shape, despondent, fatigued, and angry man looking back at me. I hate what I see. Both in the mirror and in my dreams. My nightmares. Am I going to have to tell this guy, this doctor, all of it? Am I going to have to tell him how, some days, I do not get to have a coffee because the Starbucks is too busy for me, and the thought of standing there, in line with people at my back, is too much to bear? Or about how, when I do get coffee, I need to sit at the same place, along the table at the back of the room, so I can see all who enter and leave the coffee house? Should I explain that I hate crowds and busy places because I need to know what people are up to, and I need to be able to see their hands? Maybe I would start by telling him how I don't drive anymore, and sometimes in the dead of winter, I would rather face frostbite as opposed to being on a crowded bus with people who could pose a threat. *Jesus, what is he going to think of me?*

He turns out to be a nice man, quiet, professional, and easygoing. That doesn't change the severity of the subject matter, but it does help with navigating its malevolent waters. He asks me about flashbacks. I say, "Yes."

"How often?"

"Seems like all the time . . ."

He writes.

After about three hours of sitting and talking, fighting back the urge to cry and sometimes scream, the meeting is over. I leave the office with a prescription in hand. It is a heavy piece of paper.

~

THE END OF MY MILITARY career was anything but illustrious. By early 2008, I knew deep within my bones my time as a soldier was coming to an end. I had become an administrative nightmare, as told to me by my chain of command. This was in direct contrast with how my military career had started. I had been a good soldier, a great shot, and a skilled medic. Had you met me that April, you never would have known it. I was arriving late for formation, falling out of line with relation to disciplinary actions. I was even caught lying on one occasion. I had arrived late to work and told my superior I had been stuck at the bank. I had no interest in telling him I had been suffering from nightmares about Boomer and the awful rattle heard on the day I carried his remains. I was also plagued by constant strife at home within my relationship. Conflict at home and sleepless nights did not provide breeding grounds for proper decision making. As such, I began to fail.

I was a liability to go on my scheduled tour. I was seriously distracted, thinking about loose ends when I needed to focus on the important tasks at hand deployment demanded. Overseas, other people's lives would depend on my abilities, and it was prudent for everyone that I decline because of my current state, giving Colin an opportunity to get moved up to this deployment instead of his scheduled one.

The next month, May, I was at the garrison, standing in the back of a dust-coated military ambulance, taking inventory of expired and damaged supplies. The overhead sun beat down in a relentless and punitive manner. A cascading beam of light broke its way through a petite-sized hole in the top corner of the back of the ambulance, searing a permanent scar into my memory. Dust particles danced in defiance of gravity through the laser-like pillar of light.

As a private and I rummaged through medical bags and cabinets, discarding expired supplies, a deep voice broke in from behind us. We spun around to meet whatever commands awaited us from our sergeant, a kind but disciplined man. "Relax. Take a seat."

He stood at the back of the ambulance with squinted gaze beneath the boasting sun. What followed was a painful reminder of our chosen profession we were in—he spoke with unrehearsed empathy. "A man is dead."

I sat and listened intently to the message, incredulous. My eyes struggled to remain unencumbered of tears. It was not simply a man who had died, it was a fellow medic, a friend, a brother. The sun watched Corporal Michael Starker die that day, and now it peered through the back canopy of an aging ambulance and watched as a little piece of me did as well. I fought against every instinct to break and wail.

"Take the time you need, pull yourself together, and then come inside. I will break the news to the unit post-lunch."

"Yes, Sergeant."

The sergeant turned and walked away. I remained manacled to the bench seat in the back of the ambulance. The private tried to speak to me, but I shrugged off his attempts. Filled with anger and grief, I barked, "Shut up!"

The sun followed me for the next few days. It followed me home and then to the bar. It rose the next morning, slapping me and my hangover in the face. It tailed me to the funeral hall in Calgary, and it continued to mock me from above when I stood graveside as part of the honour guard (what would be my last official act as a Canadian soldier), watching as my friend was lowered into the earth.

The heat from the sun permeated our pristinely pressed green uniforms. It laughed as sweat greeted tears and melted into the collars of our shirts. It hung above as if perched on a throne, watching as peons grieved and mourned the loss of a man. The sun was bright, but the birds were silent. Only heat could be felt, and only the bereft clatter of rifle rounds overhead could be heard.

After Starker's funeral, my problems with sleep did not ease. Fights at home escalated, and my issues with command did not lessen. One morning prior to walking through the main doors of my unit, I made up my mind; I was going to resign from the army. A decision I hated but felt necessary. I stood in front of my sergeant and explained to him that I was failing in my duties—a statement he deemed an understatement. He agreed I needed to leave his army. He was all too eager to sign the papers, even have them expedited so my release would happen faster. It is a process that can take up to a year. For me, and much to the enjoyment of my sergeant, I received my honourable release papers in July, a mere two months after having handed them in.

My time in the army was brief and brilliant, terrible and amazing. I did not get to leave the way I wanted to. I also failed to leave as a whole. But I did manage to leave with a hole, a cavernous wound within my soul.

I am a flawed man. There are things I would have done differently. And there are things I would not change. I will also be forever proud of earning the right to wear the flag upon my shoulder.

I was once a soldier, injured by an invisible round fired from a gun unseen. The lesion it left is still healing. It has been infected for a long time.

# CHAPTER 12

# Civilian

It was a Sunday, a beautiful Sunday in July, barely two months after Starker's death. My girlfriend and I had just arrived at her family's farm, and we were looking forward to a brief reprieve from the brashness of city life. Her father's land carved itself into the rolling dunes of the Alberta landscape. It was a little over an hour away from the city, so it was quiet, peaceful—juxtaposed with what we were used to from living in the downtown. I remember the sun transforming itself into a brilliant orange as it began its slothful descent. It was nearing dinnertime, but the patio looked too tempting, so we did away with tradition and opted for a liquid repast instead. We all sat around the patio table and conversed lightly, swapping the occasional joke. I noticed our beverages were running low, so I offered to head in and procure some more "dinner" for us all. I excused myself from the table and went inside.

As I entered the gloriously air-conditioned house, my phone clamoured to life. Startled by its sudden burst, I reached into my pocket and withdrew it. Looking at the screen, I was perplexed. It was the number of the military base back in Edmonton. I was confused because I had been released from the army two days prior. Why were they calling me? I answered. I pressed the phone to my ear and greeted whomever was on the other end of the line. It turned out to be one of my former commanding officers. He was telling me I was to return to the base as soon as possible for a unit briefing. I was now confused. I informed the commanding officer I was no longer in the army and I had my release papers signed a couple of days ago. There was a brief pause before the voice on the other end told me to "disregard." He told me not to worry about coming into the base and to forget what he had said. Without even saying goodbye, the line went dead.

This unnerved me because it felt like the commanding officer was using an outdated call list to bring everyone back to the unit for an important briefing, meaning something bad had happened.

I felt this way because the only time this type of command was given to those within the unit was when one of us had been killed. This is what happened when Boomer died, and it is what happened when Starker was killed, and now it was happening again. The only difference was I was no longer a soldier and consequently not invited to the gathering. My stomach began to churn.

Having been released so recently, I knew plenty of medics still back at the unit as well as those currently deployed. I picked up my phone and began calling one of my friends who was still serving. Julian was his name. The phone cycled through its familiar ring a couple of times before giving way to the sound of Julian's voice. He greeted me with a tone that reflected how my stomach was feeling. "Julian, buddy, what the fuck is going on?"

"Henny, I dunno yet, man. They just called everyone back in. I was golfing."

"Shit! Bro, as soon as you know . . . please?"

"Of course, brother. Fuck, of course."

And with that, we hung up. I placed my phone down on the island counter and stared at it, wishing it to come to life with news of what happened. It only took a few minutes for a call back, but I managed to live and worry a lifetime in those moments. By this time everyone from outside had noticed my prolonged absence and made their way inside.

"Matty?" My girlfriend's voice travelled from the doorway to my ears. It caused me to spin my head while simultaneously picking up my now ringing phone. I had an audience peering at me as I began to learn the shattering news of what had happened. On the other end of the line was Julian; his voice stammered through a couple of failed sentences. But eventually he was able to string together a coherent revelation of agony.

"Henny, I'm really sorry, man . . . It's Colin. Colin is dead. Wilmot's gone."

There was now a brief and unspoken silence between Julian and me. I was no longer confused; I was crushed and still crumbling. *That was supposed to be my mission.* I felt my knees buckle and vibrate as if they had been hit by a hammer. I am not even sure if I said goodbye to Julian before releasing the phone. All I recall was placing it down on the counter and taking a moment while ignoring the inquiries from my girlfriend and her family. Eventually my head sluggishly turned toward them; they had not moved from the doorway. I felt my eyes begin to burn as my brain came to terms with what had happened to our dear friend. To our brother. A tenuous wall of tears now sat along the lower lids of my reddening eyes. Though I had spoken not a word, they all knew something awful had happened.

"Matty . . ." the voice was now muffled by a haze enveloping everything. My mind suddenly started sprinting into the future; it thought of all the newscasts soon displaying a small picture with the likeness of my now fallen brother, informing the world that Canada had lost another one in a land far from home. The country would see a picture and read a headline, whereas I would see my friend. My dear, dear friend. Colin.

The trance broke when my girlfriend, who was now standing right beside me, started tugging on my arm. "Matty, talk to me. What is it? What happened?"

"I . . . I . . ." Speech failed me, just as it had Julian. I choked on a few more vowels before revealing the heinous news. Just as my words began to fall, so did my tears. I spoke through grieving hiccups. I managed, "Colin . . . Colin's dead. Colin's dead!" What followed was a silent audience and a wailing man. There was a physical pain attached to my skin with each exhaled cry. I was rapidly devolving into an inconsolable child.

Never in a million years did I think Colin would be killed. A man with the heart of a fucking lion belongs in this world, and he was a man with the heart of a lion, make no mistake. He practically begged for the opportunity to deploy: a once-a-day trip into the commanding officer's office to state his case of worthiness. He pleaded for the mission. There was no fear or hesitation with him, only determination and grit.

Like many soldiers, Colin was made up of different elements. There was the funny, eclectic goofball whom we all knew and loved, followed by the consummate professional dedicated to his craft. There was also the pragmatic learner and the humble teacher. A man of discipline, both with regard to military structure and the world of martial arts. Colin was basically a PG action figure who flirted with an R rating when needed. He was loyal, kind, and philosophical, too. I couldn't help but remember that night we went out and unwittingly chatted up commanding officers.

Colin was a hero and warrior in every sense of the word. It has been said that he was even telling the infantry how to save him after he was hit. A stoic medic in the field of medicine. An incredible teacher, even in death.

My first official act as a civilian was to receive word about another brother who had been killed in the land of sand and stone—a man I felt had taken my place in line when I had failed.

What did I do in the army? I said goodbye to three great men—men of unmatched calibre. I served my country and failed to honour it all at the same time.

# PART II

# THE SECOND JACKET

Men's
Size: Large/Tall
Shell: 100% Polyester
Colour: High-visibility yellow, multi-pattern reflective

THIS JACKET WAS ISSUED TO me as new. It came embraced by a plastic sheath, a fabricated placenta, if you will. It symbolized a medic born. The vividness of colour was intimidating to the naked eye: "high visibility," indeed.

When I remove this garment from my closet where it now hangs superfluously alongside other items, the colours boast less life. The magnificence of new has given way to the etchings of experience and time. To the untrained eye, this may seem like any other work jacket: speckled with dirt and grime, stained with the unknown, and well utilized over many years. But to my eyes, this simple coat and its woven fabrics hold a story of love and loss. Hearing the fibres sing against themselves as the jacket rustles in my hands is what tells its tale. You see a jacket. However, I see a portal through time and space—tactile time travel.

A uniform is a funny thing. On its own it becomes merely a random garment, easily lost among the slain laundry on the floor. But when worn or viewed by its wearer, it becomes a map of places travelled, sights seen, and experiences lived. Pieces of me are tightly woven into the very fabric of the deep navy blue and reflective yellow. I have lost an innocence and a blissful ignorance after seeing the world through my uniform's painfully clear eyes.

I sit on the couch, and although I am dressed in a simple man's button-up, blue jeans, and boots, I feel the ghostly weight of a jacket once worn in the pursuit of preserving life—*ut aliis sit vivere*—so that others may live.

CHAPTER 13

# To Be a Paramedic

IT IS LATE AT NIGHT, or early in the morning, depending on how you choose to tell time. I am in my apartment, playing an online game with a good friend of mine who lives in a different city. I am wearing my headset so we can chat and play our video games, my ears completely covered by the padding and soundproof earpieces.

All of a sudden, I hear a tremendous clatter. It sounds like thunder rising from the ground, very different from the usual passing of heavy transport trucks or street cleaners. This is something else entirely.

It is so intrusive. I remove my headset and wander over to the window. I glance out, looking to the right and then to the left and back to the right again. Nothing. But now I hear a faint hissing sound from somewhere on the street. I toss a shirt over my head, slide on a pair of shoes, and exit my apartment.

As I enter the humid night air, I am instantly met by an odour not easily mistaken: gas, natural gas. I am baffled. I descend my rickety stairs to the street. I take two steps, and I see a man who appears animated and passionate about whatever he is discussing with whomever is on the other end of his cellphone. My gaze pulls away from him as it draws to the sight of an overturned vehicle, a four-door sedan. It is resting on its hood and windshield. The car must have smashed into one of the gas metres that hug the buildings along the other side of the street. The hissing intensifies.

A catastrophic display of metal and plastic carnage lies along the road and lines the sidewalk, leading directly to the vehicle with skyward-pointed tires.

I am not sure how many people are inside the car, or if the man on the phone was involved. A quick survey of his crisp white shirt and stylish designer jeans leads me to believe he is merely a passerby, a concerned citizen. I make eye contact with him and yell, "9-1-1? You on the line with 9-1-1? You good?"

He says yes. I instruct him to step back away from the area as the natural gas is still violently hissing into the air. The smell is prevalent now.

My mind and body are recalling the skills I used as a para-medic, the competence exercised at times like these. It's instinct. I begin robotically and methodically assessing the scene and its surroundings, looking for all the hazards and scanning to see who is a rubbernecker and who might need help. The scene is not at all safe. I know that. But I need to know how many people are inside the overturned vehicle.

I angle myself so I can see into the car. I can't get too close because of the gas and the mangled unit that used to house it. I need to know, though. If there is anyone still trapped inside, are they alert? How bad are their injuries? Can I even help them? I don't have an ambulance or the tools within. All I possess is a working knowledge of what needs to be done.

As I allow the orange fluorescent lighting of a nearby street lamp to be my guide, I round the back of the car and can now see what is inside. There is a single male occupant in the driver's seat. He is upside down and his arms are dangling to the roof, which is now the floor. I continue to round the back of the sedan, scanning to look for things such as airbag deployment, intrusion of bent metal into the vehicle, smoke, or subtle flames. These are all things I need to know.

The driver begins to speak. He looks right at me. He motions for me to come nearer. He is shouting, but that damn hissing—I can't hear a word. Instead I tell him, "Help is on its way."

Against better judgment and safety protocols, I go close enough to almost reach inside the driver's side door. The glass was smashed out in the commotion. It is everywhere. It is like being surrounded by a violent glitter. The ominous hissing sound grows louder with each passing second. Despite the gas-laden air around me, a new scent begins to emerge. It is billowing from inside the car: alcohol. It is so potent that, for a brief moment, it actually overpowers the smell of the gas.

Through a veil of blood crowning the occupant's forehead, he continues barking at me. I cannot understand what he is saying. I realize it is because he's placing the letter "s" into words that do not need them. I am not able to carry on a conversation with him. I reassure him that help is on the way and that I'm not going to leave, but I need to get some distance between me, the gas, and his overturned car.

I jog back to the other side of the street where my apartment is and dial 9-1-1 myself. With expertise that only comes from experience, I explain to the dispatcher what has happened. I feel calm and collected.

While I am on the phone, more people passing by come to realize something has happened. A group of men attempt to pry the door open. They refuse to listen to my warnings and fling the door wide, releasing the inebriated man from his crashed reality.

I watch as he staggers along with them to a nearby lawn. Feeling like I should attempt some type of assessment and inform all parties they should move farther from the area, I walk over. I place myself in front of the injured man, who is now sitting upright on the grass. I call out to him, and he struggles to look at me, not so much because of the injury, but because the alcohol has drowned his coordination.

He begins to speak through a jumbled mess of rushed words. I am once again hit by a plume of his alcohol-filled breath. As I look at this bloodied and glassy-eyed man, a sudden rush of remembrance comes flooding back to me. I feel each and every drunk driver call I have ever attended as a paramedic. I begin to freeze. I no longer feel in control. The scene is no longer mine (not that it ever was), and the man, this slurring man, is no longer a patient, but rather a trigger of past experiences.

One by one, the calls come hurtling back to me. He begins to cry, and that, too, brings with it the incessant screams and pleas of those trapped behind mangled metal amid noxious fumes. I am quickly becoming a person in need of help myself. I take this as a sign that my "work" here is done and return to the other side of the road.

I stand by my apartment, cloaked in the shadows of the night, thinking I am out of sight and removed from danger, all danger. I am not.

I begin to hear the nearing wails of emergency crews. I feel a tap on my shoulder. *Damn. I let my situational awareness go to shit. How could I allow someone unknown to me get close enough to even touch me?* Another cardinal rule broken.

My head snaps around, and I am now looking at a blonde-haired woman. She appears to have been out tonight as well. Her unsteady wobbling and the 7-Eleven hot dog firmly clasped within her left hand are telltale signs. She asks me, "What happened?"

She speaks with her mouth full, and I begin to paint images of the dead upon her face. Not by choice but compelled by injury. My injury. My injured brain simply chose to do it. I feel sick to my stomach. I walk away without saying anything. I retreat deeper into the shadows of my alleyway. I squat by the brick wall and allow my back to rest against the jagged surface. Bowing my head, I catch it with my hands. Tears come. Only a couple manage to sneak past the defences of stubborn refusal, but a couple is enough.

I jump to my feet and angrily swipe the tears away with my thumb. As I do, a firefighter walks past on the sidewalk. She must have noticed me because she enters the alley and says, "Hey. Do you live nearby?"

I motion with my right hand, pointing upstairs to my building.

"Okay. You should go inside. If we need to evacuate the area, we will come and let you know." She turns to walk away but pauses. "Are you okay?"

I hesitate because I want to say, *No. No, I'm not okay.* Instead I reply, "Yep. I'm fine."

I go back into my apartment, close the door, and wander into the living room. I think maybe I can watch some TV to distract my mind a bit. However, when I look at the TV, all I can see coming from behind it is the spastic array of flickering red and white lights.

I explode into a fit of crying on the floor. I weep and I weep. I get angry and I shout. I abuse my pillow with a flurry of screams and obscenities. I feel defeated, weak, and lost. I once had the ability to care for others as both a soldier and then as a paramedic.

I can't sleep. I am exhausted, though. I am tired of being tired. I am tired of being so broken and feeling weak. I am ashamed of who I have become after having been who I once was. I have worn the uniforms of heroes, and I have had the honour of knowing many. Tonight, however, I am nothing more than a man who hides in the shadows and wipes tears away from his cheeks.

I grieve the man I used to be. I sit and contemplate my journey from army medic to civilian paramedic.

~

In what was supposed to be a celebratory month of my release from the armed forces, things quickly disintegrated. Colin was dead, my unit was still deployed, and I was in a failing relationship, all the while freshly removed from all that was once familiar and safe. If I were planting a garden designed to encourage alcoholic growth, I most certainly had the required fertilizer.

On top of all this, I still needed a job. My hands—my mind—knew how to do only one thing: to be a medic. Having no clue how to go about finding paramedic work, I quickly began scouring the Internet for jobs. I was fortunate enough to see that a small rural town was hiring and threw my resume in immediately.

Shortly after, things progressed rather positively and with haste. I got the job. I began working long stretches of country roads and farmlands, picking up injured travellers and workhands alike. It was a good introduction to the uniqueness of civilian medicine.

It was a great place to start, but it wasn't where I wanted to stay. Working for this small-town ambulance company involved working four straight days and nights away from home. This did not help alleviate any of the tension between my girlfriend and me.

Fortunately, the city service opened up its hiring portal online. I applied instantly. I would go through the arduous process of interviews, physical fitness testing, medical adaptiveness, and topographical knowledge-based exams, all in hopes of getting the job. After several weeks and months of waiting, I got the call. I was now a paramedic for a major city I had ridden out in once before.

Back when I was still in the army, I remember being told by my petty officer that I was going to be riding along with city paramedics as part of my pre-deployment and maintenance of clinical skills. I was excited to get back on the ambulance—first time since my practicum. The night of my first ride-out, I had no idea who I was supposed to be meeting. So I stood in the kitchen area of the ambulance station in the city's north end, awkwardly shifting my stance from side to side as medics paraded in and out of the building for shift change. Finally, a tall, sturdy man with a commanding yet obviously kind presence walked up to me.

"Matthew?"

"Uh, yes . . . sir!"

"No, no. Greg. Call me Greg."

"Sure, yeah . . . Greg."

He extended his hand to meet mine. Although his shake was firm and authoritative, it was not at all intimidating. I was to shadow Greg over the next several days and nights. I didn't know it then, but there was no one better.

Greg took me to the back of the rig and showed me around the ambulance, giving me a tour of their equipment and supplies, asking me how much of it was in use within the military where I was currently serving. It was all there. Greg seemed pleased with my humility and eagerness to learn, and we got along well.

Now, years later, I was excited to be hired by the same service where Greg worked. I would once again encounter the big-hearted man. He seemed larger than life to me. His voice carried a deep timbre, which was soothing to those who knew him—and commanded immediate attention from those who did not. I was eventually stationed at that same ambulance house where I had met Greg those years prior. We even worked on the same truck, albeit on different platoons. He was on nights when I was on days and vice versa.

On numerous occasions we would exchange pleasantries and guffaws while standing in the oil-stained ambulance bay. We became Facebook friends, no longer just colleagues floating past one another at shift change.

When that day came, the day where I responded to the bad thing, the *really* bad thing, Greg was there to hear me out before I went home. I sat on a bench outside the station, and he forwent his responsibility of signing on merely to make sure I was indeed okay. I will always remember his compassion, because I wasn't okay even though I said I was.

A year or so later, I tried to return the favour and altruism he had gifted to me on that bench. It was now he who had been to a bad thing, a *really* bad thing. His heart hurt. At least, that's what his message told me. I replied by telling him to stay positive and offered up my company anytime he wanted to have a beer and set the world right. He thanked me, and then I never spoke to him about it again.

# CHAPTER 14

# Dildo to Dispatch

I AM IN A QUEUE inside the mall. I am standing in line, agitated as I wait for the sales associate to stop flirting with the handsome figure ahead of me. I hate malls. I don't do well with people. Put those two things together in the same place, well, that's just the worst.

"May I help you?" a man asks. I am pleased to find a second salesperson standing before me. He must have either come back from break or just started his shift. Regardless, I am all too eager to say yes. He smiles and attempts to make small talk as he leads me to a computer monitor.

I need a new phone because mine suffered a catastrophic malfunction—and by catastrophic malfunction, I mean I threw it against a wall when I was angry.

"So, what can I do for you today?" he asks.

"I . . . uh . . . need a new phone. Mine is a tad broken," I inform him as I try not to look guilty.

"Well, I'll be happy to help you. Can't be without a phone, can we?"

"Right? I mean, how else am I going to yell at strangers online while posting funny cat videos?" He smiles again. I do, too—slightly.

We speak on and off as he navigates his computer screen in an attempt to get me the best possible deal, or so he claims. It is of no matter to me, though. I need a phone and had already prepared myself to pay far too much for a piece of plastic, glass, and circuitry I am ill-equipped to understand. He does his thing, and I continue to hate every second I am in this place.

Malls are reverberant, and people are loud. This is not a good combination for me. I do my best to calm myself, but it is difficult. As I lower my head in wait of further news from my busy helper, I hear the mall's overhead PA system crackle to life: A muffled voice echoes throughout the winding labyrinth of consumer traps. As the voice drones on, I find myself beginning to smile. A real, hearty smile. Something about hearing a dulled radio voice—it makes me think of dispatch.

~

BACK WHEN I FIRST STARTED working for the small-town ambulance service in rural Alberta, I arrived for my first shift. My partner, a seasoned paramedic by the name of Witter, was a brilliant medic with a modest and comforting aura. Although I was admittedly nervous about the shift, I was somewhat relieved knowing my partner for the next few days was going to be Witter.

This was my first job after being released from the forces, and I was still adjusting to civilian life again. I was about as green as any paramedic could be. I remember walking around, addressing each one of my colleagues as sir or ma'am just as I had done in the army. I am sure I appeared as though I had something prickly and uncomfortable firmly planted up my ass. I was nervous and awkward.

Witter was the class clown. He was able to take the edge off almost any situation. On this day, he quickly did so by cracking a few jokes and then whisking me off on the ambulance coffee run, a coffee run I did not know I was paying for. Rookie tradition, I suppose. The way Witter moved around, bounding with a goofy gait and joking with almost anyone who happened to cross his path, made me feel more and more at ease. He also had an intensely contagious laugh. Whenever he would snicker at one of his own jokes or at the reactions he was getting, it was almost impossible not to join in. Soon I felt like just another guy on the truck.

Our shift was four days long. It was a series of two day shifts, followed by two night shifts. Over those four days, we would respond to a handful of calls, none of which I recall all that clearly now. I assume they went well. I do know I watched and soaked up all the knowledge Witter had to offer while on calls together. He was one medic I would feel comfortable having work on any member of my family.

It was into our last night shift, and we were standing in the ER of the local hospital, readying for a patient transfer. The patient needed to be taken into the city, and we were the crew assigned to do it. Both Witter and I were happy. First, because we knew this was a standard, low-acuity transfer, so not much was needed from us other than to taxi this person from the sticks to the urban sprawl of the city. And second, because we could now have our pick of all the best coffee shops around. While stuck at our home base station in town, coffee was procured from either the gas station or the local diner, neither of which was stellar; but coffee was coffee, and coffee is the lifeblood of any good medic.

Just prior to leaving, Witter was exchanging flirtatious banter with one of the ER nurses. She informed us that at the end of her shift she and a few of the other nurses were going to be having a house party in town. She said it was a pre-bachelorette get-together and if we were back from our run, we should swing by. We said we would love to oblige.

The transfer to and from the city went without a hitch, as did our acquisition of a decent cup of coffee. On the way back, Witter was singing badly out of tune with the radio, and I was sipping my coffee through a permanent smile. It was a great introduction into the world of working with a partner. Through an uncoordinated bobbing of his head, Witter quickly flung his hand toward the volume dial of the radio and silenced it while simultaneously announcing, "Matt, ohhh, Matty. I got an idea, kid!"

"Oh, yeah? What's that?"

"Ohhh, Matty, buddy . . ." This statement was followed by a billow of mischievous laughter.

"Let's swing by the house where the nurses are and get on the loudspeaker."

He paused while staring at me with the childish grin of a mastermind. "Let's get on the speaker like the cops do, and we will tell 'em all to come out with their hands up. I'll squawk the sirens and everything. Oh, yeah. Let's do it, buddy."

I don't think he was actually awaiting my approval, more so just looping me in on the plan he had hatched while singing and driving at highway speeds. I simply laughed out loud and uttered my agreement. After I said, "Sure," he brought his coffee cup to his lips and began to sip from it while giggling.

We got back into town a little after sundown. As Witter pulled onto the ramp, he stopped the truck and allowed me time to dismount and hurry to the rear of the ambulance to guide him into the bay. The autumn air had a crisp bite to it, but it wasn't too bad. My fleece work jacket did a good job of combating the chilly night air. The beeping of the reversing ambulance captured the attention of the other crew inside the station. They had come to see how the trip went. Before I could even begin telling them, Witter's voice broke through. "Boys! Get dressed, we're goin' to a party!"

I looked at the day crew and watched as confusion washed over them. Witter went on to explain his master plan, and it was of course told with flair. In turn, it was met with the laughter of agreement.

The day crew threw on their fleece jackets and scurried to their awaiting ambulance. Around this time, the door to the inside of the station burst open, revealing a triumphant Witter with his arms extended into the air and his mouth stretched into an ear-to-ear grin. He looked at me and said, "Rook, I have peed, and it was a hearty pee, a good pee, a pee to rival all other urinary excretions. I am ready to ride."

"Okay, sir . . . sorry . . . Witter. Let's go," I said, shoulders shaking with laughter. Witter climbed into the driver's side of the ambulance. After pressing the green button to the bay door, I took my place in the passenger's side of our rig.

The ambulance started pulling forward, and as it did, Witter's chuckling morphed into a roaring laughter. He was like a big kid. On calls, though, he was calm, cool, collected, and brilliant. The mix of the two was perfect for this line of work.

Witter knew all the streets and back roads of this town by heart, and he navigated the ambulance with precision around each corner and down each bumpy road.

Eventually, we pulled up to a quaint house planted on a residential street. The lights inside were on, but the blinds were closed. Occasionally, I thought I could see the silhouette of moving figures, but I was unable to make out who or how many people were inside. I looked in the passenger's side mirror in time to see the day crew ambulance pulling up behind us. Witter must have noticed also. Once he felt as though they had settled into position, he looked me dead in the eye, the corners of his mouth lifted high toward his brow and his cheeks inflated by a coast-to-coast smile. He picked up the mic and prepared to speak into it. I'll admit, my heart was beating with a quickened pace, as though we were about to pull off a prank of epic proportions. I was also experiencing a slight mix of anxiety, not knowing how the nurses inside would respond to the prank, especially from Witter and his rookie. There was no going back now. I was just along for the ride. As my apprehensive smile began to widen, my eyes made a shocking discovery. One that I had to quickly inform Witter of.

As Witter held the mic in his right hand, his thumb hovering atop the PTT (press to talk) button, my eyes followed the cord spiralling from the bottom end of it. They tracked that coiled piece of cable from the mic all the way to the centre console of the ambulance. That was not where the loudspeaker was plugged in. Witter was holding the mic that is used to talk to central dispatch. If he were to press down and begin speaking, he would be communicating directly to the dispatching centre. My eyes widened, and my jaw lost all muscle tone and dropped. I regained control and began to speak, trying to tell Witter that he was holding the wrong mic. "Witter, Witter, that's the dispatch mic . . ."

Just as I was saying that aloud, Witter turned to look out the window toward the house, the look of an immature mastermind still plastered all over his face. I could see his subtle reflection in his window. I watched as he pressed down with his thumb. I heard the slight click and then listened, shocked as Witter began to speak loudly into the now live mic. "Ladies, ladies inside the blue house. We know who you are, and we know what you are up to. PUT DOWN THE DILDOS AND COME OUT WITH YOUR HANDS UP!"

"Witter, dude, the mic . . ." I tried again.

"Ladies, I will not tell you again. PUT THE DILDOS ASIDE AND COME OUT WITH YOUR HANDS UP!"

Witter turned his gaze toward me after noticing no movement within the house. "Did you hear anything over the loudspeaker?" he asked, confused.

I watched as he looked outside the window one more time, and while pressing down on the mic, he began to recite his unrehearsed comedy routine again. "Ladies . . ."

I quickly cut him off, more assertively this time. "WITTER!"

Witter looked at me before peering down and noticing the loudspeaker mic securely latched onto its locking mechanism. Now as the perplexed look washed away his once jovial expression, he began to piece it all together. I could see the dawning realization rise on his face. First, he looked at his right hand, the hand that was holding a mic, the mic he had been shouting into. Next, he looked down and followed the cord, just as I had done, and began to understand exactly what I had already noticed. His head now snapped from the window to the mic to the centre console over to me and then back to the console. This was repeated several times until finally he spoke his first words since the ones he had spoken into the mic he had assumed to be the loudspeaker: "That's what you meant by 'dispatch.'"

"Yeah, dude."

"Well . . . I mean . . ."

As he was beginning to speak, a sudden and startling knocking sound came from his driver's side window. It was a member of the day crew, their expression revealing what he now feared: He had indeed spoken his commands about dildos over the line to dispatch, and everyone in a multi-mile radius had heard it.

I looked through the window to the hysterical expression on the day crew medic's face. In seeing his reaction and hearing the muted sounds of laughter break in through the glass, my smile shamefully grew wider. I was doing a good job at remaining somewhat sympathetic to my partner's mistake until . . . "Medic one. Medic one. This is dispatch . . . uh . . . are you trying to reach us?"

A hollow voice crackled in through our speakers. Upon hearing that, seeing the laughing medic outside, and watching Witter grapple with the reality of this prank gone wrong, I could no longer contain myself. I started howling, a deep belly laughter so continuous, it robbed me of all air until I was laughing silently, with the occasional wheeze escaping my collapsing lungs.

"Shit! Matty, brother, they heard it." Witter struggled to come to terms with what had happened. He began to lower the window. While doing so, the same voice we had just heard came echoing through the speakers once more. "Medic one . . . uh . . . Medic one, are you all right? Do you need police assistance? Please respond."

Witter tried to regain enough composure to respond to dispatch. At this time, we heard the distant sound of a house door opening. We looked to see where it was coming from. To my surprise, it was the house filled with nurses. They had indeed heard Witter's demands, but not over the loudspeaker. One of the nurses on call had a hospital radio set to the main dispatch channel.

The nurses now joined the day medic outside Witter's door, and we all laughed as we watched Witter turn a bright shade of embarrassed red. He began to shush everyone. While speaking through continued chuckles, he said, "Matty, you gotta talk to dispatch. They are gonna send police if they think we are not secure."

At first, I thought he was continuing the joke and making light of the situation—he wasn't. He was serious. Fighting off the giggles, I held the mic. I tried to mentally prepare myself to press the button and inform dispatch we were fine. I managed to say, "Dispatch, this is Medic . . ." before I erupted into heavy laughter.

We would eventually clear things up with dispatch. Although they never admitted to hearing what Witter had said, we all knew they had. For the remainder of my time spent with that ambulance service, this was a running joke.

# CHAPTER 15

# Ma'am, I'm Sorry

THIS MORNING I WAKE MYSELF up, apologizing. "Ma'am, I'm sorry
. . ." I say this to no one, and yet it is intended for someone very
specific.

I am apologizing to an elderly woman, a woman I have apologized to once before. After all these years, I remain unsure as to
why the interactions I had with her now late husband have stayed
with me, but they have. I can recall the events perfectly.

~

IT WAS A CALL THAT had come deep into the evening. My partner,
Frank, and I sped through the arteries of the city on our way to
an aged couple's dwelling. Not knowing what we would face once
inside, we readied ourselves for anything.

The story we were told unfolded as such: The couple was in
bed together. The grey-haired woman's husband, resting comfortably within the embrace of their bed pillows, was reading passages
from one of his books. She sat next to him, doing the same. She
heard her husband take a large inhalation of air before he seemed
to drift off to sleep. She recalled smiling at the thought of her dear
Frederick having fallen asleep while reading. In her contentment,

she continued on, reading her novel. When the satisfying weight of fatigue settled in, she placed her book down on her nightstand and rolled over to a position of comfort to allow her to fall asleep. Slightly disturbed by the dominant glow of Frederick's bedside lamp, she requested politely that he switch it off. Her pleas went unanswered.

"Frederick. The light? Please," she asked. Frederick said nothing. After many years of wedded bliss, they each knew how to effortlessly annoy the other. Thinking that Frederick was having a bit of fun at her expense or fearing he had let the batteries in his hearing aids die (again), she rolled into a seated position next to him and dug a sharp but loving elbow into his ribs to ignite him into action. Frederick did no such thing. Frederick didn't move. What she had heard was not Frederick's slumbered breath—it was his last.

Frank and I, along with many other uniformed saviours that night, would show up and stampede through their beautiful apartment. The hollow clunking of footsteps could be heard singing throughout the home as we tripped over one another and our medical supplies. She stood in the corner of their home and watched as countless sets of hands pawed her breathless Frederick.

One med, two meds, three. Compression after compression, and the pushing of one drug after the other until eventually, stillness. Absolute cessation of movement and breath. Frederick was gone, and we had to concede to that defeat. And we did. One by one, together.

There is a strong juxtaposition after running a code. At the start, an army of uniforms come rushing in—at the end, a sullen retreat occurs. It's a terrible thing to see and an even worse thing to be a part of.

First, the firefighters leave. Then the supervisor. All that remains are the medical shrapnel of a war lost, the bereft, the deceased, and me, the sorrowful medic and his ever watchful mind.

"Ma'am, I'm sorry . . ."

Have you ever watched someone's face fall apart from indescribable suffering? I have. More than once. More than twice. More times than I care to recall.

The woman started disintegrating from within, and the descent of her soul dragged her to her knees. She was now silently begging to the heavens. I have heard many people cry in my life, but I have rarely heard anguish quite like this elderly woman's. She was an injured wolf, separated from the pack in a desolate landscape. We were the moon, standing and watching.

Frank and I took a knee on either side of the woman. I placed my hand atop one of her shoulders, feeling the craggy landmarks of bone. Her body spasmed beneath my resting hand. I apologized once more for her situation.

"Ma'am, I . . . I'm deeply sorry for your loss." Her response was spoken just above the level of a whisper: "Frederick."

I stood up as the deep ache in my knee refused me any more time kneeling in empathy beside the woman. When I did, I took quick inventory of the pictures that hung on the walls of their quiet little home: Younger versions of a couple in love beamed out of rich, decorative frames throughout their place. It appeared as though Frederick had been some form of a pilot in his youth, and from what I could tell, the old woman had spent most of her life on a farm. A sad irony came to me: A woman of the earth had fallen in love with a man from the sky. The sad part? Her gaze was now firmly cemented downward. She knew where the flying man would now forever be—embraced by the earth she so loved at one time. He was no longer soaring beside her.

I always hated death notifications. In my opinion, they are one of the worst aspects of the job. I remember almost all of them, I think. I certainly remember the grey-haired woman. She knew we were there. You could just tell, but she never spoke another word to us. She got up at one point and walked over to her husband's side before collapsing once more. When the police and victim services came, we relinquished control of the scene and snuck back into the bleak cover of the night. Our shift was not over. I would find myself saying "I'm sorry" again the very same evening.

When my shift finally ended, I found myself standing waterside by one of the lakes close to my place. I was still in uniform—the motivation to change at the station had left me by the time we parked the rig. I stood as the sun began to inch its way into the sky, a tea in hand and an angry sadness within. The water was calm; my thoughts were anything but.

I looked into the sky. It flaunted the pink and orange magnificence of early morning glow. When I exhaled, I could see the vapour of my breath. I did not feel the chill, though. Regretful? Yes. Cold? No. I cast a meaningful glance toward the sky and said, "Sorry, Frederick. I tried, sir . . . I tried."

By the time I took a sip of my tea, it was cold. I went home, went to bed, slept for a few restless hours, got up, got dressed, and did it all again. That was my job. It was my calling. And although at times it left me feeling miserable and sorry, it was my duty to try. And try I did.

CHAPTER 16

# Steps

I AM WANDERING THROUGH A mall, killing time before therapy. *Why do I only remember the tough calls?* I wonder. *Why don't I remember more of the feel-good places I have been dispatched to.* Probably another symptom of my PTSD. I notice the stores have their snow shovels out already, long before the season starts.

Many people hate the winter. I feel at home in it. Something about the calm and the still of it all. In the winter months, especially around Christmas, the world just seems to slow down for a while.

~

FROM THE AMBULANCE I WATCHED craggy flakes of the cotton-white sky break off and fall to the earth, blanketing the city streets in a brilliant alabaster. If it wasn't for the uncomfortable embrace of my body armour, I would have forgotten that I was working.

The day had been pretty decent. I was partnered with Mike Skinner. Skinner was my mentor when I first got hired on with the city ambulance. He was a lot like Greg in that he was an astonishingly smart paramedic. I enjoyed working with him, and he taught me a lot.

Best piece of advice he ever gave me: Treat every patient the same way and always start with A, B, C—that way you'll never mess up. The second best piece of advice he ever gave me: Pack a lunch.

"Matty . . . hey, Matty." Skinner's gruff voice pulled at my ears. I must have been daydreaming as I watched the wintry world around me. It was as if I had a real-life snow globe outside my window.

"Yeah, what's up?"

"Coffee?"

"Sir, that would be lovely."

The ambulance jostled into gear and the back tires struggled to find traction through the ever-mounting snow. The streets were barren; it is was as though we had an entire city to ourselves.

Skinner was an experienced medic who had worked many a shift in weather such as this, so there was no chance of us getting stuck—especially when on our way to procure coffee.

*Ding-doo, ding-doo.* Our radio went off; we had been snagged for a trip. Coffee would have to wait.

I read the display screen and relayed the information to Skinner. After ploughing through new snow, Skinner had completed the U-turn and was now steadily steering toward our destination. The information about the call was innocuous enough, nothing too sinister. In fact, it came across as an alpha response, one of the lowest severities of calls a medic could be dispatched to. That doesn't mean it might not turn out to be emergent, but currently it wasn't.

Skinner drove with skill and ease through the pristine lake beds of city snow. My eyes took passing snapshots of my surroundings. Christmas lights adorned almost every home in town, boasting mesmeric crimsons, royal blues, and emerald greens. The cascading crystals took on the colour of whatever flickering light they floated past on their way down to the bed of flawless white.

"Okay. This looks to be the place. Let's grab our shit, see what it is."

"Sounds good, Skin. I'll nab the monitor."

"10-4. Grab airway, too."

"Copy."

After picking up what was needed, we ascended five or six snow-laden steps to the front door of this sleepy and modest home, now covered in ankle-deep snow. Skinner pounded on the door to announce our presence. I continued to survey what was around me—lots and lots of snow.

The door groaned its way open and an elderly woman stood on the other side. She was crippled and hunched over by kyphosis and struggled to even make eye contact with us as she could only raise her gaze so high.

"Hello, ma'am. Name's Mike. This is Matthew. We are with the ambulance; did you call for us?"

"Oh . . . yes, dear. I need some help, you see."

"Okay, well let's see if we can fix what's bothering you. Mind if we come inside?"

"No, no, please. Come in."

A warm juxtaposition greeted us from inside the home. It might have been cold and blustery outside, but inside it was warm and vibrant with love and care. The entirety of this place smelled liked baked delights and cinnamon candles.

"So, what seems to be the trouble?" Skinner inquired.

"It's my fault, boys. I am sorry to have called. I just can't . . . I can't, you see . . ." An elderly man's voice spoke up from the corner of the room. A tired, kind old man was tucked away beside a Christmas tree near the rear of the living room.

"I'm sorry, sir. What can't you do? Are you hurt? Sick?"

"No, no. Nothing like that. I'm just too damn old."

"Oh, Jerry, stop that. You're perfect the way you are," the woman chortled affectionately.

"Ma'am, can you tell us why we are here today?" I asked while lowering myself slightly to alleviate the burden of her having to strain to look up.

"Well, it's just that . . . it's just . . ." she started.

Jerry continued, "It's just that we are stuck, or will be. That snow is really coming down and I don't get around so good any-more, ever since my fall last year. I am just afraid that we will get stuck in here and should anything happen to Maureen, well . . ."

"Oh, you silly old fool. I'll be fine. He wanted to see if you would be able to help us shovel our steps and our walkway. He just can't, and sadly I just don't have it in me."

It occurred to Skinner and me both: This old couple had no one else to call, so in fear of being snowed in (which was a very real possibility with their limited mobility), they called 9-1-1. Although maybe not the best use of emergency services, we were it, all they had.

The couple looked on as Skinner and I digested what was unfolding. In this moment of contemplation, I noticed a wave of shame befall the couple. It was palpable. They felt bad for having to use an emergency number for something that at one time in their lives would have been effortless for them. Jerry struggled to get up from his chair.

"Boys, I am really sorry to have troubled you. Maureen and I, we will be just . . ."

"Do you have a shovel?" Skinner asked. Both Maureen and her Jerry looked at Skinner and me, their faces covered with the competing expressions of embarrassment and gratitude.

"A shovel? Why, yes, yes, I think we do."

"Great. We'll need that."

"Oh, are you sure? I mean . . . I am so sorry to have called. It's just . . ."

"Ma'am . . ." I said, bending at my knees a little more now. "It's no issue. We'll dig you folks out." I reassured her with a sturdy smile.

Mike and I got to work. We worked against the relentless snowfall. We each went over one another's shovelled paths to remove as much snow as possible. We did the best we could, and it did look a lot better than it once had, but the snow was not letting up. Nonetheless, we did what was asked to the best of our abilities.

This wasn't a completely uncommon thing, being called to something like this. I have seen on the news another medic from out east doing something very similar for another elderly couple. I won't lie, thinking about that news story and then placing it next to the sheer relief that now emanated from the couple inside made me feel pretty fantastic.

We finished and informed the friendly duo that the work was done. We double-checked to make sure they were not in need of any other medical care. Before we left, Maureen appeared, carrying a tray of freshly baked cinnamon rolls.

"Boys, you simply must stay for a roll and some tea," she announced.

Skinner and I smiled at one another. "Ma'am, we'd love to. But our shift isn't over. We have to get back in service. Is there anything else, anything at all, you need before we go?"

"Boys, boys, you're good boys. Much appreciated."

"Sir, merry Christmas. Ma'am, merry Christmas to you," I said, tilting my head.

Skinner and I left and went back in service. We never did go and grab coffee. If you ask me, it's because we were already warm enough on the inside.

# CHAPTER 17

# Uninvited

I AM STANDING IN LINE at the Starbucks near my place, and it is busy. There is a sea of clamouring voices: some sharp, some soft, and the occasional rumble of a man's bass. Slow-moving coffee seekers are strewn haphazardly, awaiting their beverage of choice. I am trapped within this chaos. There is a woman behind me. I know this because I am always aware of what and who are around me. She occasionally reaches into the sandwich bin beside me, sifting through and struggling to find what it is she is looking for. So far it is tolerable. I am not really affected by any of these happenings. However, in her zeal, she uses one arm to push against me—not hard or forceful, but uninvited. She then lurches into view from my periphery. This causes the same startle—fight or flight—as my shadow often does. I react. Badly.

"What the fuck are you doing? Why are you touching me?"

Her eyes melt into a befuddled gaze. She says nothing. In my mind, scurrying patters of inquisition and indignation slam into one another. Anger begins to fill my veins. All I want is to pay for my tea and go for a walk around the lake. Instead, I feel as though I am under threat. Sweat drips down my back. My palms clench inward and become bone beaters. She has scared me. Her innocuous act has caused absolute fear to pollute my blood in an instant.

All things around me stop. No more voices. No more busy hands. Just eyes. And all of them are stapled to my skin. I can feel them crawling over me. I am overcome by shame and embarrassment, so I leave. No tea. No peaceful walk around the water.

Events such as these happen with enough repetition that sometimes it feels safer to just hide from the world. Avoidance, I have been told. Not a reasonable tool, apparently. It is exhausting—living within two worlds simultaneously.

~

As WE WALKED THROUGH THE doorway, our workboots thumped against the aging linoleum floor. Before we made it to the end of the hallway, the ominous sounds of a woman crying and pleading grew eerily louder. I saw a man lying on his back in the living room. A woman who looked worn was kneeling beside him. Her face was stained with running mascara, and her hair was in disarray. When she looked up at us and realized who we were, she began barking orders. "Hurry the fuck up!" There was another figure in the room, sitting on a smoke-stained chair off in the corner, close to the TV. It was an older woman. She appeared to be almost emotionless. She just sat quietly with her lit cigarette, watching the madness unfold. This whole scene was just weird: a man lying motionless on the floor, an unhinged woman shouting orders, and a suspiciously quiet elderly lady smoking her cigarette while watching TV.

My partner, Dean, and I attempted to get to work, but the woman who was giving orders refused to move. She remained in the way, obstructing us from helping the man on the floor. She started pawing at me and pulling on my utility belt, trying to drag me down to her crouched level. I don't enjoy demanding, uninvited touches. To her dismay, I removed her grip on me with a moderate amount of counterforce.

"Could you move so we can get to work?" I asked.

She did not budge. Her agitation was incessant and escalating. "You are doing nothing. Why aren't you doing anything?"

I tuned her out for a moment and peered down at the man on the floor. He appeared lifeless and was beginning to wear a haunting blue around his lips. I knew if we did not intervene soon, whatever hope this man had of returning to life would diminish. I asked once more, this time with an authoritative tone and posture. "MOVE OUT OF THE WAY," I asserted.

I was met with tears and angry snarls of non-compliance.

"I have had enough. If you don't move, I will have to move you. We need to access the patient."

I began squeezing one of the many pressure points located on the inside of her arm, while forcibly removing her from the victim. Needless to say, she appreciated this even less. I could smell the stale beer and tobacco on her breath. She was now hurling insults at me.

A group of firefighters were now on scene, and they took over as an almost human shield, preventing the woman from staggering back toward me and the man on the floor. Although, I will admit, her focus now seemed to be solely on me.

I knelt beside the patient. While my partner managed the airway, I began searching for an IV site. During the unavoidable interactions with the uncooperative woman, my partner had attached the man to the monitor and readied the airway kit. The monitor as well as physical confirmation showed he was alive and had a heartbeat, but he was not breathing. With urgency, both my partner and I began voicing aloud, "What did he take? What drugs has he taken?"

A voice came from the corner of the room. The lady in the chair responded stoically, "That is my son. He has taken some of my Oxy as well as heroin."

I was able to place a quick IV in his arm. As I was taping it down, I could still hear the venomous scorn from the woman who had once been kneeling where I now was. But suddenly, her angry hurling of insults gave way to the readying of spit. She forced the saliva to the forefront of her mouth and, through pursed lips, let loose a sniper shot of mucus and tarred sputum. I was not facing her at the time, but I felt it land along the back of my neckline and the collar of my shirt. A frenzy between the spitting lady and fire-fighters now ensued. I didn't have time to deal with her directly, so I was happy to have the support.

I did have words for her, though; they incensed her even more. She managed to snake her way through the flailing arms of the firefighters with catlike aggression and thrust her foot deep into the side of my ribs through a series of kicks as she continued hailing spit.

Miraculously, around the same time as this was going down, the seemingly dead man on the floor shot up from the ground into a seated position. The speed at which this all happened was enough to cause a fleeting silence to fill the room, even from the spitting woman who was now being escorted out of the house by a couple of pillar-sized firefighters. The man removed the adjunct we had put in to keep his tongue from occluding his airway. Through a deep expression of confusion, he stated, "I'm good. Shit, thanks guys . . ."

We hadn't even given him the Narcan yet. The combination of high-flow $O_2$ and respirations had provided his oxygen-starved body with enough motivation to come back online. Not for long, though. He would drift in and out several more times until we eventually gave him the Narcan.

Feeling like he was all right (and against medical advice), the man ripped off all of the electrodes and removed the IV. He proceeded to barrel through the house and out the door, disappearing in the blackened city streets. It was a strange call, indeed.

~

WHEN I ARRIVE BACK HOME from the coffee shop, I feel a little safer in my apartment. However, I continue to stew in my own thoughts about the day. *How can I ever show my face in that Starbucks again?* I will have to find a new place to get my tea.

Later, I decide to go to bed relatively early (early for me) and try to capitalize on my body's intention to rest. I fall asleep quickly, but it is too good to be true. I am forced awake at three in the morning. I am fighting the woman from all those years ago yet again. This time she is not present. My body thrashes within the sheets, struggling against the imaginary adversary, except this time there are two enemies: the woman and my own PTSD-laden mind. I am brought into consciousness, still feeling her foot in my ribs. I place my right hand onto the back of my neck to wipe away her spit. It, of course, is not there.

Being attacked comes with a huge adrenaline dump and the adrenaline woke me up. My pillow is on the floor. It must have taken on the form of the woman while I was sleeping. Yep, I kicked my pillow's ass.

Matt: 1

Pillow: 0

I take some time to calm down, trying to slow my breathing and acclimatize myself to the here and now. I will try once again to catch some sleep. I can only hope there is no round two with my pillow.

# CHAPTER 18

# Walls

I SIT WITHIN THE WALLS of my apartment, playing some online games with my friends and my brother. As per our nightly ritual, I wear a headset and we converse with an upbeat and enthusiastic tone on a wide range of topics. Eventually, though, the night of gaming draws to a close, and video game machines are turned off, headsets removed. My mind begins to wander.

My apartment is silent. Absolutely free of noise. Even the refrigerator ceases its buzzing. I begin to hear a subtle sound emerge: me breathing. Deep, concentrated inhalations, followed by a sudden release, and then repeat.

I enjoy the camaraderie of gaming. As my ears register the cadence of my breath, my wounded medic's mind transports me back to another time when, as a paramedic, I was surrounded by work colleagues and stories. It was a challenging job, to say the least. But then I remember a story, a good story, a funny story, early in my career.

~

AS A PARAMEDIC WITHIN A city service, you are exposed to all manner of things: some good, some bad, and some hilarious. There was one night of the latter I will never forget, no matter how hard I might try.

I had settled nicely into the welcoming embrace of the station chair yet remained cautious and suspicious about the unusual slowdown in call volume.

We had been steady, don't get me wrong. But by this time in our shift, I had managed to eat all my lunch (while it was still hot), take an uninterrupted bathroom break, and enjoy a warm tea. Now I was reclining in a cushioned lounge chair for longer than fifteen seconds. This was a mythical situation in the first responder world.

It should then come as no surprise that I envisioned the EMS gods lying in wait, readying to unload the most grotesque, incomprehensibly heinous of calls upon us at any moment. And to make things worse, Mike, a medic on another rig parked at the same station, flippantly commented, "Boy, sure is quiet out, huh?"

I threw my balled-up gum wrapper at him, and my eyes bored holes through his innocent, befuddled face.

Of course, his naïve statement was enough to tickle the listening ear of said gods and allow them to conjure whatever they so desired. And with that, our pagers went off. Mike and his crew were sent toward the downtown; Frank and I headed to a well-known retirement complex in the city's west end. As we each pulled out of the ambulance bay and onto the ramp, I glared toward an oblivious and happy Mike. We parted ways, moving toward our respective destinations.

The details from dispatch informed us we were responding to an elderly female complaining of chest pain. The notes scrawled across our screen also indicated that this individual of advanced age held a rather variegated cardiac history. Frank and

I donned our thinking caps and readied to do battle against the malevolent will of heart disease.

We pulled up on scene, and my eyes were met with the familiar stone and brick structure.

"Welcome to the Octogenarian Club," I muttered beneath my breath as I exited the passenger side of the ambulance. We grabbed our gear and began to traipse inside. I looked at the face of my pager and read its notes as to which apartment we were to head to.

Of course, top floor, last fucking room on the right . . .

Hearkening back to my days in first response, the calls were always located at the farthest and most inconvenient spot from where you were currently situated—last room, top fucking floor, always.

Frank and I lugged our weighted gear in and out of the elevator and then zigzagged our way down a series of switchback hallways until finally we reached the doorway of the apartment. I knocked assertively and called out, "Paramedics. Can you let us in?"

I could hear the shuffling footsteps of what I knew to be an elderly person scurrying toward the door. After several seconds of moans and whimpers of exertion, the door swung open, and a kind old man ushered us into his home.

He pointed with an unsteady hand and requested we make our way toward the dimly lit living room. It was hard to see our surroundings, but I could tell this was a well-looked-after place filled with love and a thriving quality of life. My eyes began to grow accustomed to the lack of lighting. I could now make out a frail figure sitting on a rocking chair in the back corner of the room. The wavy curls of her white hair were the first thing to catch my eye. She did not appear to be in overt distress and was watchful of our movements as we drew nearer to her.

"Hello, ma'am. I'm Matthew. I'm with the ambulance. Do we have another light we can switch on here?"

"Oh . . . ah, no dear. The lighting has burnt out and our son hasn't been able to come as of now to fix it. I can see if we have a flashlight or some candles if you need them. Monty, go get some candles, would you?"

"Oh, no ma'am, that's not necessary. We have flashlights. We'll make do. Tell me a little bit about what's going on this evening?"

She proceeded to explain that shortly after dinnertime her chest became stricken with a heaviness that had matured into a dull ache over the several hours in between then and now. She stated that she had taken "the pills" (Aspirin) as directed to her by dispatch but had felt no relief. Having had a heart attack in the past, she was growing increasingly more fearful that she might be having another. Frank and I listened as we pulled the necessities from our kits and readied our assessment tools. As she continued to speak, I began to place ECG stickers onto her chest, explaining what I was doing as I went. I wanted to take a picture of her heart as the story sounded ever more sinister to our medics' ears.

I coached this amiable elderly woman to remain still and to try to relax as I let the ECG monitor do its work, showing us what was happening within her ailing chest. A few moments of silence passed, and then an electronic buzz of ECG paper being printed filled the room. I placed my flashlight under my chin and used one hand to tear the strip away from the monitor and then flattened it with both hands to read it. Fortunately, I did not see anything evil lying in lurk. That being said, it's always good to have another set of well-trained eyes take a second look. As such, I raised my hand and aimed it toward Frank, who was standing just off to my right and about a foot behind me. There was absolutely no reaction to my waving hand. I shook the paper again to get his attention. Nothing. I shook once more, harder this time. Nothing.

This puzzled me: Frank was not often inattentive, if ever. I turned my head to see what was going on behind me, and I could see Frank standing exactly where I had known him to be. My hand was still outstretched, awaiting his collection of the coiling paper. It was at this moment I noticed Frank was not ignoring me on purpose as much as he was fixated on something else. I witnessed an expression I had only ever seen a handful of times when working with him: the saucer-eyed stare of outright wonderment. My curiosity increased and demanded I follow his transfixed gaze.

I followed the ethereal line between Frank and whatever had him hooked. This led me to the wall closest to us. Or rather, the bookshelf resting against it. It was a massive thing, wooden and compartmentalized through and through. This did not help explain Frank's fascination with it. To me it merely looked like a regular, albeit well stocked, bookshelf. I snapped my head back toward Frank and called out to him. Without twitching a fibre, he responded as if in a trance, "Matt . . . what is this? I think it's . . . it's . . ."

"Bro, it's a bookshelf! Something you wanna tell me? You good?"

"No, dude . . . it's not. It's just not . . ."

I turned back again and now chose to follow the circular beam of Frank's flashlight. It was slowly cascading from left to right, up and down, along the bookshelf and its contents. And that's when I noticed what he saw: There, out in the open within this well-aged couple's home, stood a triumphant structure erected from floor to ceiling, east to west. It was a bookshelf that held within it nothing other than porn. Porn! I mean, magazines, movies, DVDs, VHS tapes, CDs of categorized, era-divided porn.

From the untamed lady bushes of the 70s to the landing strips of the 90s through to the immaculate hardwood of today—porn. And there it was, unabashedly on display beside this hunched-over old lady.

When enough time had passed, our patient became alerted to our hijacked attention. She then reached to the table beside her, outstretched her hand, and retrieved her dentures. I could hear the slather of saliva and the collision of plastic against gum-coated bone as she manoeuvred them into place. And then she spoke. "Oh . . . yes . . . well, that's pornography, boys." *A few cycles of elderly breathing.* "I . . . I used to be in the business, you see. Was really quite something . . ."

Frank and I shifted our disbelieving, wide-eyed stares in unison and began to take in the situation unfolding before us. This woman, as sweet and soft-spoken as any grandmother has ever been, casually speaking about how she'd won gold in the schlong Olympics; and she was smiling about it. I know this because her teeth were not in all the way and began to fall.

We continued with the call, with only the occasional pause to once again allow our eyes to ingest this lady and her wall of porn. Once we got downstairs and into the ambulance, I became a little more focused and task oriented. So much so, I became aware that the ambulance had not yet started moving toward the hospital. I called up front to Frank to inquire about status, and I was once again met with silence. Having less patience than when I was inside, I leaped through the slit separating front from back and poked my head into the driver's seating area of the truck.

"Frank, what are you doing?"

"Dude, I looked her up online . . . She's in magazines . . . This is messed up . . . We just picked up a porn star and it's not at all how I thought it would be!"

"Yeah, twelve-year-old me is heartbroken, too. Let's go. Wait, is that her?" I asked, leaning farther into the cab and closer to the screen of his phone.

"Dude, yeah . . . right?"

"I'm so confused right now. Please drive."

And off we went.

As paramedics, we see some things. We really do.

The elderly lady was fine, by the way. And by fine, I mean her *heart* was fine.

~

BACK WITHIN THE WALLS OF my apartment, the gaming console is shut down. *Should I try to sleep? Should I read?* I am not sure of what to do, but reflecting back on that story, I can tell you what I DON'T do: watch porn.

CHAPTER 19

# Burning Flashbacks

I SIT NESTLED SAFELY IN Doc's office. It is therapy day. She is speaking, and I am listening. Until I am not. In an act of mutiny against sanity, my aching mind twists the fabric of time and space, bringing the events of the past into the realm of the now. I am in the middle of a flashback.

I begin to smell and taste smoke. I feel it brush against my skin with its sinister embrace. In my mind I am in an apartment, waiting for a patient. I can no longer hear Doc. Her office has burned away from view. I now hear the roaring flame, the snapping hiss. I am sitting in the real world all the while burning in another one. Agony. I can hear the sirens getting closer. They are so loud.

~

THE BUILDING WAS ENGULFED BY flames, licking themselves high into the blackened sky. A truly sinister sight to see. My partner, Denise, was an older, experienced medic. We did our best to park at a safe distance away from the blowing wind. It was futile; the heat from the roaring blaze permeated the ambulance. Where a campfire's sound is serene and calming, an uncontrolled structure fire is nothing short of crumbling chaos.

It's mesmerizing in the most terrifying and hypnotic of ways. It sounds like nature screaming a horrendous war cry.

I exited the ambulance and walked carefully but dutifully toward the fire captain. I made our presence known and indicated where the ambulance was located. He acknowledged my directions with a decisive nod and then returned his attention to the growing adversary before him.

Ashes and soot landed around me like falling snow. The first time I was brushed by fiery ashes, it was in the form of a flake falling on my forehead. Almost dead centre. Unlike a snowflake, it didn't land with a cold, wet embrace. It was, instead, a feeling all its own—it landed softly with an unwieldy violence. I used my hand to wipe it away, remnants of streaking ash staining my fingers.

I began walking away toward the ambulance when my radio came to life with a muffled and metallic voice of panic. It was one of the firefighters from inside the raging building. "Cap, we got one. We're coming down the stairs. We need medics ready now!"

I started running, my mind processing what I had just heard. Denise must have heard it, too, as she was now outside the ambulance, fetching the stretcher from the back of the rig. I grabbed the gear I thought we would need, threw it onto the stretcher, and ran to the burning building.

The top floors were now nothing short of an epic inferno. The closer we got, the more the winter's night air gave way to the heat of that conflagrant hell.

We were ushered in by ground-crew firefighters and led into the lobby. It was explained to us that the rescue team was bringing down the patient. We had no other information other than that we were about to be busy. At this time, my partner called in for a second ambulance, which would later turn into a third and then a fourth.

Out of my right ear I could hear the heavy thuds of the over-encumbered firefighters descending the stairs and coming toward us. There were about four of them carrying what looked like an ash-soaked man. The narrow construction of the stairs, along with the healthy bodies of the firefighters and their gear, made for a less than graceful descent.

When they neared the bottom of the stairs, my partner and I reached in and relieved two of the firefighters of their carrying duties. I wish I hadn't. When I reached in, the only thing available for me to grab onto was the wrist of the injured man. The weight of his body would see that his charred and blackened skin would peel and slough off. Much of his skin remained stuck to my hands.

The whole encounter was executed with skill and haste, but it is amazing what the mind can snapshot in those fleeting seconds. As I reconfigured my grasp in readiness to hoist this man onto our stretcher, I could see he once sported a beard, a beard that was now fire-bitten. The smells from that night were punishing and ubiquitous.

Despite our best efforts, the man would die. My only hope was that he had lost consciousness before all this damage and pain. In my head, I fabricated a story where he had had a heart attack and was unresponsive before the fire even got to him, but the reality is I will never know. The only certain thing was he died that night as the fire continued to roar.

At the end of my shift, I went home as if it had been any other day on the ambulance. I carefully and quietly unlocked my front door, entered my home, and ascended the stairs to the bed I shared with my girlfriend. I followed my routine of walking into the room, not turning on a single light, and almost tip-toeing so as not to disturb her. A foolish practice when part of my routine was also going over to her side of the bed, gently brushing hair away from her face, and kissing her softly as if to say, *I made it home. Another safe shift.* She would moan and sometimes even smile.

"Matty? Why do you smell like smoke?"

"Ah, there was a bad fire tonight. Go to sleep, I'll tell you in the morning. I gotta go shower. Love you."

"You, too," she muttered.

I never really talked to her about my bad calls. At least not in detail.

I entered the shower and turned on the water. I stood beneath the stream and allowed it to rinse the nightmare off me. Blackened water rolled off my skin and swirled through the drain below. I was covered in the lingering reminder of untamed fire. Ash and soot were being cleansed from me. Likely remnants of the patient as well.

The water continued to pour from overhead, and I did my best to steady my mind so I would be able to go to sleep. I heard the sliding-glass door of the shower open. My girlfriend joined me.

When all was said and done, we found ourselves on our bed with her head on my chest. She was breathing softly and drifting to sleep. Me? I was picturing a fire, burning with a limitless rage and barbarity, and my forehead still felt its kiss.

~

IN HER OFFICE, DOC BEGINS to guide me back from the flashback. She uses her voice like a beam of light, cutting through the dense wall of blackened smoke. She says my name softly, asking me to tell her what is going on. Upon hearing her question, more of me returns to the chair in the office. The smoke evaporates, retreating to the darkened place of memory. The flames leave, the sirens are now absent, and I have returned to the now. And as much as that sounds like a good thing—and it is—I am now confronted by another adversary: shame.

I hate feeling so fragile. I used to be asked to enter the areas of a city that most pretend don't exist. I was also asked to go into the darkness that no one knows about—and I did, willingly. But not anymore. Not today. Probably never again.

# CHAPTER 20

# Paper Rose

I AM WALKING AROUND MY neighbourhood. It is raining. Normally I love the rain, but it is pouring heavily so I decide to seek refuge in a nearby bar, a modest booze-scented sanctuary.

"Hey, there. What can I get you?" the perceptive bartender asks.

"I'll just take a lager, thanks."

"Sure thing."

She smiles and lets her eyes linger a moment as she steps away. I don't get the feeling she is flirting with me out of interest. This woman is light-years out of my league. No, I think her motivation is less about me and more about tips, and rightly so.

When I was in the army, the government paid good money to ensure I became as highly trained as possible, moulding me into a lean, green, life-saving machine. However, I was also gifted unsanctioned lessons from those who commanded the respect of experience. One night, while sitting around a wobbly bar-top, a senior instructor told me to pay attention to what he was about to show me.

"Heneghan, look here . . . pay close attention. This is gonna help you out immensely with the ladies. 'Cause let's be honest, your face ain't doing you no favours. Watch closely."

What unfolded or folded, rather, before me was a napkin. A twist here, a fold there, wrap once, and *voilà*: the napkin rose. It really was a thing of beauty.

Now, years later, I am still adept at creating the flower. I stealthily remove a napkin from the edge of the bar and proceed to fold it into a paper rose. When the server returns with my beverage and places it down in front of me, she smiles and says, "There ya go. Enjoy."

I reply with both a thank you and the unveiling of my freshly crafted paper napkin rose.

"Oh. My. God! How did you do that? Do you just carry those around with you?" She seems genuinely impressed.

I smile. "No, I just made it. Figured you brought me a beer, so the least I can do is this . . ."

~

DURING NON-LIFE-THREATENING EMERGENCIES ON THE job, I would often find myself in the company of our ever-aging population. Sometimes they just needed to hear that everything was all right, or maybe just someone to talk to for a while. Seniors make up one of the largest call volumes medics deal with. One day during the late autumn, I was dispatched to a well-known seniors' living facility for an elderly woman with chest pain. My partner, Frank, and I began rushing toward the scene. Chest pain calls are always dispatched as a lights-and-sirens response because of the potentially serious nature of such a complaint. We whisked in and out of stagnated lanes of traffic through the downtown core until we had reached the upscale housing complex.

"You know, when I age out, this is the kinda place I want to be held up in," Frank said while tilting his neck backward, visually taking in the mammoth structure of the building.

"Yeah, it's nicer than most on the market, that's for sure."

I felt the cool brush of a fall breeze press through my fleece jacket. I shivered for a second. We grabbed our gear and began making our way through the opulent hallways of this lavish establishment. As per usual, the call address was on the top floor, farthest apartment from the elevator.

We made it to the apartment and noticed the door already cracked open for us. I knocked just loudly enough to be heard and announced our presence to whomever was inside. After peeking past the door itself, we noticed two thin-framed old ladies sitting in the living room. One of the women had her hand on her chest. The power of observation told me this was our patient.

"Hello, I'm Matthew, I'm one of the paramedics. What seems to be going on today?" I said as I pressed farther into the room. I knelt beside the lady. She began to speak. "Well, I seem to have woken with this awful pressure on my chest, and it just won't go away. I thought I had better call and have this looked at."

"I see. Well, let's see if we can't help you out with that. Can you tell me a little more about the pressure?" As she spoke, I proceeded to place ECG stickers onto her arms and legs as well as her chest. She informed us of her complex medical history and her previous heart attacks. She was a nice woman, kind and soft-spoken. I could see that she was putting on a brave face, but from behind the veil of stoicism, it was obvious that this situation was troubling for her. I always did my best to ease the tension in scenes such as this. I figured if I didn't look worried then maybe the patient would feel as though they shouldn't be either.

Frank and I continued to investigate and formulated a plan for the patient. We knew she should go to the hospital and have further diagnostic evaluations conducted, and we relayed this to her. She reluctantly acquiesced. Frank radioed to dispatch for a hospital destination, and I readied both our gear and the patient for transport.

While I was doing that, I turned to the second elderly woman in the room, a friend of the patient. I began to make small talk in hopes of diffusing the obvious tension in the room. Both women seemed to appreciate this. The second woman, Patricia, spoke fondly of her friend and requested that we take good care of her. I assured her that we would, and she nodded in appreciation.

"Ma'am, would you like to come with us to the hospital?" I asked Patricia.

"Oh, me? Oh, dear . . . I don't think I can. I have a hockey game to go to later this morning."

Without missing a beat, I responded, "Oh? Well, that's terrific. What position do you play?"

There was a brief pause at the casual nature and delivery of my question. It was obvious the grey-haired woman was far too old to be playing any sports, let alone hockey. I allowed my mouth to form a mischievous grin, demonstrating that I was joking. With that, both ladies erupted with laughter.

"Oh, goodness, no. I am far too old, you silly man. I am going to watch my grandson. He is playing today . . . Cheeky man, you are."

"That's what they tell me," I said.

"Mildred, you make sure he behaves himself on the way to the hospital, dear."

Mildred smiled, and another round of lighthearted laughter bounced off the walls. We helped Mildred to our stretcher and proceeded to head down the hall to the elevator. As we did, some of the other residents of the housing complex began to emerge from their respective apartments. They all looked on with worry as Mildred passed in the hallway. I could see more trepidation peeking through the brave face she so gallantly wore for us.

"So, since Patricia plays hockey, that must mean you're what, a linebacker?" I teased. She returned my question with a toothy, buoyant grin. Other than reassuring her that all was well, there was not much else I could do for Mildred. The real work of finding out what was happening to this dear old lady would come from the doctors and nurses at the hospital. So I did what I could to make her feel as comforted and cared for as possible.

I rode in the back with Mildred on the way to the hospital. We joked and swapped stories. She told me of her late husband and how she missed him very much. She wished her children could come and see her more often but understood life could be busy sometimes.

When we got to the hospital, triage informed us of a current bed shortage. We would have to wait in the hallway for the time being with Miss Mildred. We parked the stretcher along the wall. Frank took a coffee and tea order from both Mildred and me, and we waited.

A hospital can be an unsettling place at the best of times, let alone when you are the one strapped to a gurney with an unknown health complaint. Mildred bore witness to a screaming man who was brought in by another crew while escorted by the police, a paramedic crew performing CPR on another elderly person, and a psych patient who was in obvious need of sedation and monitoring. She tried to appear brave but her eyes betrayed her. Mildred's apprehension was palpable.

I noticed a Kleenex box off to my right, resting atop another stretcher. I reached over and withdrew a single tissue. I engaged in small talk with Mildred while holding the tissue within my hands. A twist here, a fold there, wrap once, and *voilà*: the paper rose. She was mid-sentence when I presented it to her. Her mouth slammed shut, and she began to investigate what I had just handed her.

"My word, is that a . . . That's a rose."

"Yes, ma'am, it is. And it's for you."

"For me? Oh, you . . . you kind boy."

She was smiling once again. She twirled this simplistic tissue rose in her fingers. You could almost hear her smile. Those moments made the job feel indescribably rewarding. A simple act of kindness can change the world for someone else. I was not able to rid her of the ache in her chest or fully alleviate the fear she felt by being at the hospital, but I was able to offer a momentary distraction from those things.

# CHAPTER 21

# The Boy

I STARTLE AWAKE TO A shrill scream and a bone-rattling plea for help. It is the wee hours of the morning. At first, I think the noise is coming from the hallway of my apartment building. I remove myself from my bed and wander over to the door. I unlock it and peer into the hall. All I am met with is the sight of an empty hallway, humming softly with the sound of overhead fluorescent lighting. I close my door and retreat back into my apartment.

The cries continue. "HELP! PLEASE, HELP!"

The screams permeate my hearing. This time not as a sound from outside my door but as a distant wail from just beyond reality. I realize I am having an auditory hallucination. The screaming I am hearing is not coming from a living person. It is coming from a memory courtesy of my contaminated mind. It appears as though my mind is once again oozing its poison into my consciousness. Conceding to the fact that the blood-curdling screech is merely a fabrication of a brain plagued by PTSD, I make my way back to bed. For the next hour, I toss and turn. It is too late. I am already beginning to burn from the inside out: anger.

I rip the covers off me and walk toward the kitchen, my feet thumping along the hardwood flooring. Begrudgingly, I flick the light switch and grab some water. *Great. Now I am too angry to sleep.*

Sometimes I think the screams are the worst. Especially when I know who they belong to—or rather, who they belonged to.

~

THE DAY HAD STARTED OFF innocently enough—a couple of non-emergent runs to the hospital and a cyclist who had suffered a fall from his bike, boasting a rapidly inflating knee.

My partner, Frank, and I were in the city's north end. Our home station was not too far away, but it wasn't quite home-time yet. We generally liked to drive around the city as opposed to cementing ourselves to the confines of a station. Besides, born from paramedic superstition, we were less likely to get tagged for a call if we were moving around the city like a target—harder to hit while in motion. Trust me, sometimes it worked.

Frank meandered through the city streets, main roads to side streets, pushing us ever nearer to the coffee shop. I could feel the vengeful heat of the sun break in through the window in spite of the gale winds of our air conditioner. It had been an ungodly hot day. This, of course, was made worse by the fact that our bodies were snugly enveloped by our ballistic vests. Having to wear body armour on days like those, you often questioned how much you really valued personal safety. Apparently enough to keep wearing the damn things.

I felt the ambulance lean heavily to one side as Frank turned the corner and into the parking lot of the coffee shop. Frank pulled the rig into a row of parking spots and angled us into a position that allowed for a quick exit should it become necessary. Frank was an experienced paramedic and one of my favourite partners.

Not only was he a take-no-shit kind of medic, he also was incredibly intelligent and good at what he did. That included getting coffee.

"Want anything?"

"Yeah, sure. Grab me a tea, yeah?"

"Yessir. Two milk?"

"Aww, Frank, you know me so well."

"Eat shit. I'll be right back . . . love you."

I could see Frank chuckling at his own sarcasm while he walked away from the ambulance and into the coffee house. Feeling slight trepidation about how close we were to the end of our shift, I tapped the surface of our touchscreen display and took inventory of the calls actively going on throughout the city. Things were picking up—not a good sign.

I didn't want to go on another call. Having to do so would guarantee our venture into overtime, and I was sweaty, uncomfortable, irritable, and ready to just go home. There was a beer calling to me from inside my fridge.

The sun continued its relentless saturation overtop the city, and I could feel its fiery invasion bursting in through the side window. I was leaning farther and farther into the centre of the ambulance in a futile attempt to seek refuge from the scathing heat when the chimes began to emit from our centre console. As I feared, we were getting nabbed for a call.

I slapped the EN ROUTE button, which annoyingly called out from the illuminated screen of our display. I looked out the front window of the rig to watch as Frank walked back with quickened pace. His pager would have gone off to let him know of our fates: overtime.

The driver's side door groaned with a metallic wail as Frank pulled it back and entered the vehicle. He pulled the sunglasses from his face and looked intently at the screen to see what type of call we were going to. So far, all that had popped onto our screen was the address (which was shockingly close to where we currently were) and the level of severity: an echo call—the most serious of call levels.

I grabbed the mic from just beneath the centre console and asked dispatch for further information. After a brief pause and dead air, a small voice broke in from the perforated holes in our speakers. It told us of the anguish we were going to: "Alpha one-four, Alpha one-four, you are going for a suicide by hanging. Brother trying to cut him down. Active suicide. We'll get police rolling on this, too."

"Send us another unit also, dispatch." Frank threw those words into the mic as he spun the wheel with one-handed aggressive circles to manoeuvre us out of the parking lot. Before I had a chance, Frank ignited the sirens, piercing my ears and the air around us. We began navigating through stalled columns of traffic while trying to traverse the main artery of the north end. I said we were close, and we were. The call address was only a couple blocks across the major road we were currently attempting to cross. Traffic was heavy.

Frank was skilled and was able to prevent any prolonged delay by swerving in and around the blocking walls of vehicles. Once we reached the other side, I heard the growl of our diesel engine evolve into a roar with our increasing speed. Frank flew past one side street and then one more before turning sharply to the left and onto the road we needed to be on. Once we were on the correct patch of concrete, the address of the house we were responding to was about midway down.

We had driven to an otherwise sleepy section of residential homes, all seemingly related to one another by way of architectural design and appearance. The house we were going to, however, held something vastly more sinister inside than its generic exterior implied. By the time we put the ambulance into park, curious neighbours had begun to emerge from their suburban sanctuaries and onto the first step of their homes. They gaped at Frank and me as we rushed toward the home.

I saw that a side door was open, and as I pulled nearer to it, I could hear panicked voices stumbling over one another. This was the sound of devastation—easily recognizable to an ear bitten by its timbre before.

I was now outside an open door leading into the family home. On the inside there was a small row of three or four steps going up into the kitchen, and to the right of the door was a set of wooden steps spiralling downward.

As I entered the home, I took a fleeting glance at the three figures who stood trembling at the top of the kitchen stairs, deep in their own thoughts. I deduced they were the mother and father and some kind of relative to the boy.

I began to descend the steps into the basement, and as I did, I could hear the echoing thuds of my weighted footfalls colliding with the wooden planks of the stairs: *clunk, clunk, clunk*. One step after the other, down I went.

In memory, those steps seemed to grow in number and transform into a rickety escalator. In reality, there were about twelve, maybe thirteen, steps leading us into the sublevel of the boy's home.

When I reached the bottom of the stairs and felt the cracked cement floor meet the sole of my boot, I peered over my left shoulder and into the belly of the basement to catch sight of something that remains glued to my eyes to this very day—a frantic young man with a face contorted by panic and worry. He was outstretched on his tiptoes with his arms ascending upward while trying to feverishly sever whatever grasped his loved one.

I could hear him struggling for gulps of air as he sawed futilely with a plain steak knife. The sound of flimsy serrated metal biting into fabric soon became the only thing I could hear.

Instinctively, I let go of the medical bags and rushed over toward the young man and the suspended boy. I began to raise my arms in preparation to reach around the youth's legs and lift in hopes of alleviating the cinched neck of the dangling boy.

As I did, I now found myself with clasped arms around the boy's thighs, just below the buttocks. My face was pressed into his groin with nowhere else for my nose and mouth to be. Unbeknownst to me, the boy had wet himself during his deadly suspension act. As such, my eyes, lips, gums, and mouth now burned with the irritation of urine.

Frank soon came in and freed the boy from the rope's dangling embrace. I helped Frank lower him to the floor, and we instantly got to work. I used my trauma shears to slice through the centre of his shirt from waist to sternum and then ripped the remaining fabric free from his body to expose his chest. I began compressions as Frank readied the other gear. I awaited further instructions from Frank as I pressed heavily up and down on this boy's undeveloped chest. I could feel his ribs pop beneath my hand—a feeling I can recall to this day. And I did all this while continuing to inhale the remnants of foul, lingering urine. It felt as though I was swallowing tainted acid one gulp at a time.

By now other first responders had started to filter in. A firefighter took over compressions as I readied an IV line to insert into the boy's arm. When I was connecting the tubing together, I couldn't help but notice how skinny this boy was. Each rib was easily identifiable and defined. His Adam's apple bulged from his now bruised neck. He looked familiar to me, eerily so.

When I was around fourteen, I was small—tall but skinny. You might even say underdeveloped. I also boasted a protruding Adam's apple from my neck, and at fourteen I also wanted to die.

Growing up wasn't always easy for me with my mother's fluctuating health and mental state. Some days she was manic while other days she was absent and hidden under a swath of blankets. Every morning (morning being relative to whenever my mother got out of bed) I watched as she ingested handfuls of prescription medications. This ritual repeated itself at night. In the evening, though, those pills would make my mother lethargic and aloof to her surroundings. On more than one occasion I had watched my mother's hand-held cigarette deplete away into a drooping mess of loosely compacted ash on the floor of our home. This was a sight I hated growing up.

I also hated how pills seemed to rob me of time with my mother. Because my father was taken away, Mum often played both parental roles when able. When unable, coping was up to me and my nonsensical adolescent brain—a brain that once told me it would be easier to deal with the pain by taking handfuls of my mother's prescription pills while hiding in the bathroom. At fourteen, I wanted to die. I wanted the pain of adolescence to go away and the horror of my mother's cancer to leave and never return. Pills and a forever sleep seemed so logical in the moment.

I sat on the edge of the bathtub and coddled a mosaic of tablets and capsules within my hand. *Take them all. Do it right*, my fourteen-year-old voice whispered nefariously from within.

I never did take the pills. The sad reasoning behind why I didn't? It was not because of an emerging epiphany. It was because another whisper entered from within, and it told me my mother would be so angry that I wasted some of her pills. I was afraid of getting in trouble. Isn't that fucked?

As we worked on this poor young kid, I found more and more similarities between us. He was wearing blue, the blue shirt I destroyed, my favourite colour. At least, it was—until I saw the blue that coated his lips. Not a fan of that shade of blue now, not at all.

We worked and worked but to no avail. The boy was gone. Dead and lying at my feet with tubes, wires, tape, and bruises defacing his body. His left arm, the one I had started the IV in, rested on top of my boot. When I caught sight of that, I felt angry.

It was Frank who finally spoke. "Well, fellas, we did what we could, okay? . . . Doc says to call it. He's gone."

None of us said a goddamned thing, but Frank knew we had heard him. The boy was indeed dead.

"I'm gonna go up and tell the parents. You guys want to clean up a little down here? They might want to come down and see him."

"Do you want me to come with, Frank?"

"Nah, I got the supervisor with me. We're good. Sit this one out."

"Roger. I'll tidy up a bit."

"Thanks, Matty."

"Yeah . . ."

Frank climbed the stairs, leaving the agony of the cellar behind, only to wage war in a new place of tragedy—where his parents were waiting in the living room.

As I cleaned up the debris of opened med boxes and packages, I could hear Frank's voice fall through the floorboards. I could not make out exactly what he was saying, but I had a good idea of what he was compassionately telling the family. Frank and I had had the misfortune of delivering a few death notifications over our time working together. They were always different yet in some ways the same.

While cleaning up the battlefield, I couldn't help but toss fleeting glances toward the deceased boy. Each time I did, an uneasy anger boiled from within.

It only dawned on me later in life that my anger was misdirected. I was actually angry at a younger me. I was berating myself, demanding I look at the devastation I would have caused had I taken those pills all those years before.

As I bent down to pick up another piece of medical war, I heard a sudden and cacophonous boom explode from overhead. It repeated itself with sickening repetition. It was the bereft clenched fists of a wailing mother banging on the floor. *Boom. Boom. Boom.* Heartbroken artillery rounds going off. Those were the sounds of a battle lost. The realization that the reaper had won. He had bested us and taken with him a prisoner from a now distraught mother.

I left the house without ever seeing the mother or the brother again. I fled to the truck, grabbed the hand sanitizer, and hastily slapped the pump mechanism and emptied some of the foamy contents into my mouth. It was not designed for this purpose, but I had to get the bitter taste of urine out somehow. It lingered with an incredible potency. That crooning beer in my fridge at home sang much louder now.

Frank and I parted ways after that call. We filed the paperwork without discussing its events any further. In fact, we never spoke of it again.

I went home and immediately grabbed that beer from my fridge. I sat on my couch and pressed the bottle to my lips until it was time to get a new bottle, and a new one after that.

Later that night I received a call from a shift supervisor. He asked how I was and wanted to check in with me. I lied and told him I was fine. Thing is, I wasn't lying to him; I was lying to myself.

~

NOW, YEARS AFTER THE CALL, years beyond this event, it sticks with me as if it was the day it happened. Sometimes I hear screams like the ones I heard just now. Other times, when I sleep at night, I see the boy swinging in front of me. I become engorged with adrenaline and once again lunge for him. But when I do, I grab nothing but air. The boy disappears, receding into the wound of my tortured mind. My breath is replaced with a rancid taste. My tongue remembers, and so do I.

I chew gum a lot now. Every day, actually.

Here I sit in my apartment, alone with my memories. I am saddened I could not save the boy. I am saddened he did not listen to the other voice, the one telling him not to do it, not to die by suicide, not to devastate his family. That voice came too late for him—as did I.

# CHAPTER 22

# Cal and the Balloon

I AM WAITING FOR TWO friends to swing by. I met them after moving to Ontario. They are twins, a unique set of friends for me because they are not veterans, medics, or firefighters. They are just two great people, far removed from the world I came from.

We are going out for a drink or two. They are good company, kind and sincere. We head out to one of the local spots we frequent.

"Table for three, please," I say to the maître d'. We follow her, single file, to our table at the perimeter of the establishment.

I am doing my best to keep the twins rolling in laughter. They seem to have a fascination with my lighter tales of work as a paramedic.

"So, do you have any good stories for us today?" one of them asks.

As a man whose default setting is sombre to stricken, I generally fake my way through most social engagements. As such, I always keep a handful of funny ambulance stories at the ready. I find you can toss down a well-timed anecdote like a smoke bomb: You can slip away undetected while those around you choke with laughter.

We are sitting around the table, and the twins are leaning in ever so slightly in anticipation. I am feeling particularly down today, so even the hilarious stories are difficult to tell. I take a deep breath and start to share a story they haven't heard yet.

"Let me tell you about Cal and the balloon," I begin.

~

IT WAS THE MIDDLE OF a muggy summer's night in August some years ago. My partner, Frank, and I had settled into the shift nicely with the procurement of bad coffees and saran-wrapped sandwiches from the corner store. We'd been on a couple of trips already but nothing life threatening or emergent, which wasn't a bad thing considering we had a third person riding with us. Typically, an ambulance is staffed by only two paramedics, but tonight we were "voluntold" we were going to have a visiting health care practitioner on board. He was a doctor from the Philippines.

As the night progressed, our ears became attuned to our visiting medic's unique English stylings. The night got better and better when we realized his bedside manner was a little unconventional by North American standards. Cal was saying things to patients we had wanted to say for years but could not. He told the young woman in her twenties that calling an ambulance because of pink eye was stupid. He even looked sternly at an intoxicated man who was in the back of our ambulance after having been involved in a tussle at a local bar and said, "Why you yelling? It not nice. Shut up, asshole." And you know what? The guy shut up. This night was anything but ordinary, but it was great.

As the hours of our shift passed, we trio of lifesavers roamed from call to call, Frank and I partaking in the hilarity of our Filipino friend's most honest approach to patients. My stomach was sore from laughing by midway through our shift.

We were dispatched to a call for an elderly male who resided in a seniors' living home. We were told he fell out of bed and was bleeding badly.

We arrived on scene and began hauling the needed gear with us, along with the stretcher. A small-framed nurse greeted us at the front sliding doors and walked us toward the room where the elderly man was. Our boots slapped against the newly waxed floor as we tramped down the corridor. The nurse who had been leading us came to a stop and said, "In there . . ."

Cal made entry first and I followed him in. We were met by the sight of an elderly man lying face down on the cold floor of his room, an unsightly amount of blood around him and on his bed. There was so much blood it looked like he had been stabbed. We worked quickly to assess this man and his injuries. He most certainly was not stabbed or actively bleeding from any obvious injury site. And it was hard to ascertain anything from him because he was hard of hearing.

As we began to piece together what had happened, it became ever more clear that, yes, the man did indeed need to go to the hospital, but not for a life-threatening injury. It turned out that while he was sleeping, he had unwittingly rolled too far to one side of the bed and fallen to the awaiting floor. And in doing that, the catheter that had once been in place within his urethra had ripped from his penis, causing what I am sure was a frightfully painful wake-up. You see, when a catheter is in place, it is inflated by a small balloon to prevent any unwanted dislodging of said catheter. Free-falling from one's bed is a good way to render the balloon useless.

Cal was still attempting to lead the call while Frank readied the stretcher for transport. I positioned myself into place to extricate the man from the floor. Cal began to speak with the patient to explain to him what was going to happen. Now, this is where

I want you to take a moment and attempt to paint this in your mind's eye: We have Cal, a Filipino who arrived in Canada just weeks prior to this event, and whose English was less than fluent; and we have an elderly man who needed hearing aids but was not wearing any—and they were trying to talk to one another.

"Sir, you hurt. We take you to hospital."

"What?"

"Sir, you hurt. Okay? We take you to hospital for doctor."

"What? I'm not a doctor."

"No, sir. You hurt. We take you to a doctor."

"Who's a doctor?"

"We take you to one."

"What? Why?"

"Sir, you hurt yourself. You hurt your penis."

"I don't want your penis."

"No, no, sir, your penis is ow."

"Not now. No ow."

"Yes, 'ow.'"

"What?"

"Sir, pardon?"

"Why do you have my penis?"

"What? Sir, listen, you hurt your penis."

This went on for longer than I should have allowed, but I was damn near doubled over. And then, as if it couldn't get any more outrageous, Cal reached onto the bed, grasped the blood-soaked urinary catheter in a gloved hand, and held it outstretched in the air like Arthur held Excalibur and said, "Sir, this, this come out your penis. It rip from cock."

*Ho-ly shit!*

I was able to keep my composure until I heard the inevitable: a snicker of uncontained laughter from Frank. But Frank was not in the room; he was standing in the doorway behind a group of shocked nurses who had appeared at some time during the exchange. As we continued to work, the old man locked a steadfast gaze onto Cal and shot forth a hail of obscenities.

"Fuck your cock! You, penis dark man. FUCK YOU! FUCK!"

This continued in the ambulance. This continued in the bay of the emergency entrance to the hospital. This continued while in triage, and it continued when handing over care to an unsuspecting group of ER nurses and residents.

"Fuck you, penis dark man! You ripped my dick."

When all was said and done, the injured man was fine and well looked after, and Cal learned a truly valuable lesson: Never use medical terminology on a hard-of-hearing person whose penis has just been traumatized.

Cal flew back to the Philippines at the end of that month. Hope he's doing well.

# CHAPTER 23

# Sorry, Cap

I AM CURRENTLY SITTING IN a Starbucks (not the one closest to my apartment; I don't go to that one anymore), sipping on an overpriced beverage, listening to the soothing sounds of whatever jazz is playing. I can't help but question, *What am I doing here? I don't belong here*. I likely think this because, for many, many years now, I have felt foreign not only in my own skin but in my surroundings as well. Mental illness has a way of stealing your passport and leaving you stranded.

I gaze at the people around me: some smiling and engaged in banter with whomever they are sitting with, others lost in their keyboards, frantically typing away. There are also the faceless people standing in line, waiting for their order. And then there's me. Just sitting and observing, all the while feeling a gnawing thorn of remembrance burrowing its way to the forefront of my mind. I thought that by leaving my apartment and venturing out, I would be able to push it aside and have a normal day. Sadly, days spent in deep memories have been my norm for so long I guess I am being normal—*my* normal. I start contemplating the day I let the captain down.

~

IT WAS A DAY SHIFT, and we were near the end of it. We were on our way back to the station for switchover when we were dispatched on one last run. It would be one of the most difficult calls I would ever attend, a three-month-old in cardiac arrest.

I felt some relief knowing I was working with Dean, a phenomenal and skilled medic. Dispatch squawked in over our mics and informed us they were sending a second unit and fire response. On calls such as these, it was all hands on deck. As a paramedic, dealing with children was a whole other beast.

I could hear the sirens wailing through the city and down the alleys as we flew by stagnant lanes of traffic and rigidly tall city blocks. It was as though Dean could see seconds into the future and act accordingly. He zipped through halted lanes of cars and trucks as if knowing what they were going to do even before they did. This meant for a speedy and deliberate acceleration toward our little man in need.

The address took us to an area of the city with mid-rise apartments along either side of the street. They all appeared to have been designed by the same apathetic architect some years prior to our arrival. We stopped the ambulance outside an aging brick building, its numbers faded from exposure to a vengeful sun. Duct tape zigzagged its way across one of the panes of glass on the main door. As fast as my heart had been racing in preparation of arrival, it was now beating three times the speed knowing we were there.

Dean told me he was going to grab gear from the back and requested I make my way toward the apartment. I acknowledged his command with a quick nod of my head and then bounded from the ambulance to rush to the timeworn structure. I am not sure what was louder—the relentless slamming of my heart against my chest or the sudden slaps of my heels on the pavement. Either way, there was a storm brewing.

I made it about a foot and a half away from the wounded glass door when it violently swung open, revealing a woman in absolute panic. She shrieked while pushing her arms toward me as if she wanted me to grab whatever she was holding. When I dropped my gaze, I saw the baby, lying limply in his mother's trembling embrace.

I extended my hands and retrieved this precious package from the frightened woman's arms. He was so small and frail. His little frame held the tiniest of features. He was nearly weightless. Had my eyes not seen the little boy, my body wouldn't have known I was holding anything. But you know what? To this day, this baby boy is the heaviest thing I have ever carried.

Immediately upon receipt of this little man, I turned 180 degrees and began scurrying toward the ambulance. The first thing I recall hearing other than my internal dialogue was the growl of the engine snarling from our parked rig. Dean must have seen me retreating to the ambulance with the baby in hand. When I got to the side door, it was already open. Dean was standing on the top step with his arms outstretched in readiness to take the baby from me. I was in so much of a hurry that my body kept moving and forced Dean to sink backward into the working space of our truck. I bent down and placed this small boy onto the stretcher and then stood back up, never taking my eyes off him.

Soon after doing all we could within a timely manner, one of the other medics hopped out from the rig and took up residency in the driver's seat and began taking us to the children's hospital. While in transport, I was in charge of CPR. I tried and I tried; I hoped and I hoped the rhythmical staccato designed to sustain life would work.

When we arrived at the hospital, there was a team of nurses and doctors waiting for us. The back doors of the ambulance tore open even before we were fully stopped. We withdrew the stretcher that held the baby and walked briskly down the hallway of the hospital to the awaiting trauma room.

We handed over care to the team of nurses and doctors and slipped out of the room to allow them to work their magic. Outside the door, I watched as wires and tubes, machines and trollies, were placed into perfect position. Orders were given, and hands obliged. Sadly, the magic didn't work.

I was standing outside the room when they pronounced this little boy dead. My eyes fixated on his hand and how small it was. It seemed positioned in such a way as if he were asking someone to hold it.

My transfixion was interrupted by a shrill cry from down the hall; someone had just told the mother her baby boy was gone. She collapsed within herself. I could see it. Her heart sank to the soles of her feet and spilled out onto the waxy hospital floor.

The woman was taken into a quiet room along with other family members who had arrived to be with her. I wheeled the stretcher toward the sliding glass doors of the emergency bay, ignoring the empathetic stares of my colleagues. I bore a hole in the floor mere steps ahead of wherever I was walking. I didn't want to see or talk to anyone. I was sad, and I was angry.

I was shocked when my stretcher suddenly halted, causing me to gently crash into the back of it. I looked up to see what had happened. Standing there, his hand on the front of the wheeled bed, was a fire captain. He must have been on the call, too. He looked at me questioningly. He wanted to know about the baby. He wanted me to have good news—news I could not give him.

"Hey, the boy? Yeah?"

I couldn't even muster the energy for an audible answer to his query. I simply shook my head side to side.

I was taken aback to see such an honest expression of emotion from an on-duty fire captain: He began to cry. Unabashedly so. His crew must have been outside still. He raised his right hand up to his brow in what looked like an attempt to shield himself from the watchful eyes of those around us. I felt bad for him. I felt bad because what he was doing outwardly was what I was doing inwardly—crumbling.

I was burnt. Done. Fatigued beyond the possibility of replenishment. I had nothing left to give, not even empathy. I stood in his company for a moment longer, then removed his hand from the front of my stretcher and continued past him. I left him there, alone. I just walked away.

When I jumped into the back of the ambulance to restock and clean it, I closed the doors and sat on the bench seat for a few minutes. I was crying now. Everyone was out of sight. Everyone except the baby boy. I could still see his image stencilled on the stretcher in front of me.

*I'm sorry, Cap. I didn't mean to leave you.*

# CHAPTER 24

# Moving Anger

I SQUEEZE MY PILLOW TIGHTLY around my head and face, and I shout until my voice is raw. Anger, resentment, and ugly thoughts are all rampant today. Doc told me I will not always be like this, and I am hopeful I won't—but today I am just plain angry.

I hate the world and the evil within it. I hate picturing the things I have seen and done. I hate knowing what lurks in the dark corners of our cities. I hate having PTSD, and I hate feeling like I gave it to myself—like I was too weak to prevent it. It doesn't matter how often I am told it isn't my fault; I still feel this way some days.

I hate no longer wearing a uniform. I see things most people don't. My perceptions of people are distorted, and I am embarrassed. I hide from the world some days, staying inside my apartment, headphones securely attached to my ears, trying to drown out the world around me. I shop late at night, and I do laundry at impossibly early hours of the morning to avoid people. For me, wanting to scream is not a new development. I had days as a paramedic when I wanted to scream, too.

~

IT WAS NEARLY DAWN WHEN my shift ended. I made my way to a man-made lake within the city's north end. It was hidden away by statuesque trees and leaves that erupted from the wooden giants. From time to time, I would go there to decompress after being witness to the horrors the streets had to offer. I stood on the dock and rested my tired body along a nearby erected wooden beam. A mist had nestled itself atop the glass-like water. The sun was just beginning to rise, casting light on the golden leaves of the fall trees.

The setting was serene and peaceful; however, inside I was anything but. I was a hurricane of emotions, a tempestuous storm on top of unsettled seas. Chaos. I had answered the full gambit of calls throughout the night. We confirmed the deaths of two people—one old, one not so. We responded to a multitude of assaults resulting in a variety of injuries. There was an angry patient who spat, bit, kicked, and screamed at us the entire way to the hospital, and there was the rape victim—how could humanity be this depraved? It was a difficult night to reconcile. We bounced from call to call without reprieve.

As I stood beside the still lake relishing the morning chill of the crisp autumn air, I sipped my tea and struggled to make it through my breakfast sandwich. My appetite began to fade along with my resolve to stay calm. In a single moment, as if to remember every bad call all at once, every terrible instance of my military career, a whirlwind of horrible images and memories came hurtling back to marry the already despondent feeling I held from last night's shift. My body began to tingle with fury. In a split second, my hand, which held the breakfast sandwich, cocked back, readying itself as a weapon. I fired forward, hurling the sausage-and-egger high into the air, where it raced into the distance. It began to break apart as it fell from the sky, disturbing the once-flawless sheet of water.

Watching the impact zone begin to emit ripples across the lake in all directions did little to quell the fire-like rage in me. Soon, my tea joined the breakfast sandwich's fate—along with it, a billowing scream, "FUCK! FUCK! FUUUUUUCK!" Through the quiet morning air, my echoing howl could be heard bouncing off the concrete walls of nearby apartments.

Even that was unsuccessful in calming my tattered nerves. I readied my lungs to shout once more. As I began to let loose, my yell was cut short by the sight of a jogger less than ten feet from me. Her expression told me everything I needed to know about how I was being perceived. Embarrassment now permeated my tapestry of emotions. She simply ran on by but threw the occasional glance over her left shoulder toward me. I was even more ashamed of myself because I was still wearing my uniform. *Did she see me toss the innocent sausage-and-egger through the air? Did she watch as the tea spun and twirled helplessly, meeting its fate at the bottom of the lake?* If I were a turtle in that moment, I would have retreated into my shell.

My personal and professional life were in shambles. Not long after this incident, I resigned, packed up my belongings, and decided to move to Toronto. In my wake I left a house, two cats, one dog, and a girlfriend. It was the right thing for me to do.

My friend Luke and I headed east. After days of travel, we eventually emerged over the crest of a hill and were greeted by the signature of the Toronto skyline—the CN Tower. I had found my new home.

Over the following weeks and months, I attempted to heal my wounded heart by sterilizing it with plenty of outings to the bar. I met a woman named Jenna. She was kind, understanding, genuine, and sexy in equal parts. We struck up a conversation, and I surmised she was interested. I told her about the breakup.

I informed her I was a paramedic who had recently moved here. We exchanged numbers and flirted via text, which turned into a date. Jenna picked the place, as I was still finding my way. It was a trendy little bar, accented by low-hanging string lights of subtle crimson glow. She was dressed in a pair of form-fitting dress pants and a silk thin-strapped top—she looked incredible.

The evening was fantastic. We played and laughed in one another's company. We drank and then ordered more. We shared lingering bouts of lasting eye contact and unspoken word. As we walked home, the sky opened up and we got soaked within seconds. Seeking shelter beneath a storefront canopy, we waited out the deluge. While we stood next to one another, listening to the droplets of a cloud's tears, we embraced and began to kiss.

In this moment of movie-scripted romance, I realized how broken I really was—Jenna's lips didn't feel like my ex's. Her scent was different. Her hand placement off. Nothing felt the same. In fact, I didn't feel anything at all.

The rain eased, and we continued toward my place. Once home, the kissing reignited. Clothing slid from our skin to the floor. More kissing, more nothingness. Until finally a swell. When all was said and done, Jenna lay beside me with her eyes closed and her lips barely open. She was sleeping; I was not. Unlike the movies, it was not her beauty that prevented my slumber—it was fear. I did not want to fall asleep and risk a nightmare beside her. I couldn't bear the thought of that happening. Jenna was new and not yet exposed to my toxicity. I lay in bed and watched the sun glimmer to life from my window. I felt her stir beside me.

"Morning. Sleep well?" I asked.

"Mmm, yes! You look tired. How long have you been up?"

I lied through a smile. "Not long."

We went out for breakfast and saw each other only a few more times after that.

That January I got a phone call from a friend, a fellow paramedic out west. "Hey, Matt . . . sorry. I've got some really bad news. Greg is gone . . . He died by way of suicide while on shift."

The medic I had the honour of riding with to maintain my skills while in the army; the man who worked at the same station in the city service; the man who sat with me on the bench after that terrible call to make sure I was okay—he was gone, murdered by his own mind. The news hit me hard, and my nightmares intensified.

By this time, I had secured a job. But my skills and hands were beginning to fail me. I was drinking more. I arrived late for work even if it was a night shift. I knew my days working as a medic were drawing to a close. I simply refused to bite into the apple of that reality. A disquieting anxiety pervaded almost every aspect of my day: shaky hands, uncertain decisions, and physical agitation.

One night during the summer, I was scheduled to work a rave. I had worked and responded to plenty of raves while working out west. Although I held a rigid displeasure toward them, I never felt uneasy or wary. But on the night of the rave in Toronto, I threw up at least four times while on the way to my post. I had no idea why this was happening. I foolishly thought I must be getting sick and tried my best to push the trepidation out of my mind and body.

I continued to work special events as a paramedic on movie sets for several months. But my behaviour sparked concern from my employer. I eventually requested to go on stress leave, to take some time to figure things out—something I had not yet allowed myself to do since the move.

I never went back to work as a medic. Instead, I ended up on the overpass, then landed in Doc's office. I had hung up my jacket for good.

# PART III

# THE THIRD JACKET

Men's, suit jacket
Size: Extra Large
Shell: 98% Cotton, 2% Polyester
Colour: Brown

THIS JACKET IS DIFFERENT FROM any I have worn before. This piece of clothing hangs new and untainted. It is soft to the touch but holds its formal shape. The meaning of the jacket is unknown to me yet. It is not a uniform or a dressed-up variant of a uniform, it is a simple man's jacket, hickory and pecan in colour. This garment does not boast crests or rank, yet it might be the most defining jacket I will ever wear.

What I do know is this jacket represents opportunity, sobriety, and recovery for me—possibly even purpose, a purpose I thought had vanished. Is there still more of me to give? I take the garment off its hanger, and in one fluid motion allow my arms to fill the voids of the sleeves. I now stand wearing a store-bought jacket. And you know what? It fits.

# CHAPTER 25

# Perfect

I AM NO LONGER A medic. This sad reality hangs over me like a storm cloud, striking me with thunderous thoughts of inadequacy. My life disintegrates into arduous trips on the public transit system, appointments, therapy, drinking, and angry social media posts.

Tonight, after I am awakened by a horrible nightmare, I run to my computer and pour my screaming mind onto my keyboard. Anger seeps from my fingertips, and what is left is a long, seething Facebook post. I hope that in writing this, in releasing some of the poison, I may be able to go back to sleep. In a moment of disbelief, I scroll across a message someone leaves in response to my verbose bloodletting: **You should start a blog.** The comment makes me think. It might be a good way to release more of the wicked inside me, forcing it from mind to screen.

I write, and I write often about the horror in my head. The keys of my computer become the purveyors of my anguish. I sit, blinking cursor in front of me and half-drunk bottle of Scotch beside me. I think alcohol is the elixir of creativity, the needed lubricant to give birth to tolerable prose.

But today I am not writing. Instead, I wake up, have a robust coffee, and feel almost optimistic—or at least ready for the day ahead. It is a gorgeous day. The sun is shining overhead without a cloud in the sky, a crystal blue canvas for the orb to dance around on. I take the train into the downtown core and have a row of seats all to myself for the entire trip. I make it to my scheduled appointment with plenty of time to spare, have an enjoyable conversation with the person I am meeting, and leave with a smile on my face. As far as perfect goes, today is pretty much it.

On my way back to the train station, I stop and buy a hot dog from one of the vendors near the station. It is a guilty pleasure; I love street meat. After consuming the glorious, unhealthy delight, I move toward the platform—the train is on time. *Perfect.* I hop on without a care in the world. I have my earbuds in and am listening to my favourite melody while enjoying the journey back home. I notice the train skips a normal stop. I start feeling something is amiss. In my daze of serenity, I had hopped onto the express train, meaning it would fly by my stop. Nevertheless, I can walk from another stop; it is a beautiful day.

I get off and start strolling. I decide to grab a bottle of water at a corner store and have a brief rest before continuing on my adventure. After a few sips of the much-needed ice-cold beverage, and as if to suddenly come to an epiphany, I remember that the 23-bus came this way and would drop me off right next to my apartment.

I make it to the next designated stop just in time to see the bus approaching. *Man, nothing is going wrong today.* I board the bus and find a spot near the back to stand and wait for my stop. I take my earbuds out because I do not want to risk the same folly that had taken place earlier. I stand there with one of my arms clinging to a hanging yellow hand grip to balance myself along the way. Stop after stop, people board and dismount. A constant flow of human traffic. Roughly six or seven blocks from my apartment, the bus stops. An individual climbs onto the bus, encumbered by construction gear and high-visibility reflective tape. He awkwardly manoeuvres down the narrow laneway in the centre of the bus. I suck myself in, away from the aisle as much as I can to allow him room to pass, but it is of no use. His shoulder and mine collide softly, but what follows is anything but gentle. His proximity allows his body odour from a hard day's work to ferry its way to my nose. The swirling concoction punishes my olfactory system, and it pulls at my hippocampus. In the microsecond of a blink, I am having a flashback.

My nose continues to choke on this man's natural scent, and my brain starts flipping through the Rolodex of its stored traumatic imagery. It pulls forth a card from a scene I had once experienced as a paramedic, another time when I was plagued by a terrible odour. I can't stop it. This invokes such a strong response from my senses and my mind that a flashback cripples me while on a public bus. I begin to gag—once, twice, three times and then: *bleh, splat, splash.* I throw up right onto the floor of the bus. Vomit even lands on my toes peeking out from my sandals. All eyes are now on me.

The brakes screech from beneath the belly of the bus as it draws to a sudden halt. In the convex driver's mirror, I can see a pair of inquiring eyes looking back at me. The driver then peers over his shoulder and says nothing while his expression presses me for answers. I stammer through an incomplete and nonsensical response. It is at that point the driver says, "What happened?"

I fail to articulate anything resembling a proper explanation. I find myself stumbling over consonants and vowels in my mouth. I try once more but all I am able to say clearly is "Sorry . . . "

That's it; that's all I can muster. It isn't enough. The driver likely suspects I have been drinking. I must appear awful in this moment. I am asked to leave the bus. I do.

I now stand under the watchful glare of a gloating sun. I am alone and dismayed, walking along the sidewalk of the city, listening to the heavy roar of a departing bus, strings of vomit still swinging from my jaw. My wounded brain is betraying me.

I stop at a nearby establishment to splash water on my face and recalibrate my frazzled thoughts, then continue on my way. I make it home and plop myself on top of my bed, listening to the hum of the fan. I try to fight off feelings of shame, embarrassment, and fright. I begin to worry that someone may have taken a video of me and that I could become the latest online viral pass-around, "puke guy." I didn't mean for it to happen. I didn't mean to have a flashback. *God, what if I had been with a woman? What a freak she would think I am.* These are my thoughts since retreating to my secluded apartment, now my fortress of solitude.

My logical brain knows it is not my fault, but emotional me hates myself and my aching mind. I hate feeling so broken, so fragile. I hate when things like this happen to me. *Fuck you, brain. Fuck you!*

CHAPTER 26

# Orphaned

IT IS 9:25 A.M., A Tuesday in November. My phone buzzes to life, waking me while I am burdened by my everyday adversarial hangover. I clasp the cellphone and press it against my cheek. I manage, "Hello."

It is my brother Jon. I lie motionless and listen to the voice on the other end of the line, stammering and piercing through the perforated holes of my phone's speaker. His grief-stricken words are utterances I will never forget: "Matt, Mum's dead."

My mum has died by way of suicide.

I thank Jon for calling me and for undertaking such a painful task. I feel my breath sputter like a struggling engine in the middle of a winter's chill.

There is a second of silence that seems to last for at least an hour after I hang up the phone. I think all the air in my lungs collectively escapes in one fleeting gasp. I've heard people say that getting news like this is like being punched in the gut. It's not— it's more akin to having your heart ripped from your chest and discarded in the cruelest possible way. Even that explanation does not do it justice.

A few moments pass, and I attempt to gain composure. It is futile. I pick up my phone and call Doc. I struggle through a voice message, explaining what had happened and how my world had just been torn apart.

I hang up. I stumble from my bed and stammer, *"No, Mum. No, no, no, no, Mum. Please, no!"*

I blink hard a couple of times to ensure this is not just another one of my nightmares. It is indeed a nightmare, but not an escapable one. It is a living nightmare. My mum—Mum is dead. And I never got to say goodbye or I love you one last time. In an instant she is there, albeit across the country, and in the next, she isn't. She is just gone. Robbed from me. This whole thing seems unfair, like a bad joke taken too far.

I can't help it. I call my mum's phone a couple of times, half-expecting her to answer, but she doesn't . . . and it hurts like hell.

All of a sudden, I miss my mum. I miss Joan. My heart hurts with a physical pain I did not know was possible. It is surreal. It just can't be. I want it to be a lie. I want my mum.

In this moment, I would give anything to travel back in time just for one more memory of seeing my mum perched at the kitchen table, cigarette in one hand and tea in the other, silently coming to terms with a new day while letting loose a massive and unmatched passing of gas. A howitzer, if you will. That smirk painted firmly on her face, followed by, "Whoop, bloody mouse," is something I will always cherish, and now, solemnly miss.

My mother was not a perfect person. None of us are. But she loved us in the only way she knew how. With every little piece of my heart, I will miss her dearly. There were times where she was absolutely perfect. Moments where you couldn't ask for a better mum. I can still hear her laugh, even though in the last years, I heard it less and less.

~

Somehow days pass, and I manage to exist. I am sent screen shots of my mum's final note. I begin having horrid, intense nightmares about all the suicides I have ever attended as a paramedic. Of all the suicide notes I have read, I never expected to read my mother's. If this was happening to me, how was the RCMP officer who dealt with my mother coping?

I decide to call the RCMP detachment local to my mother's area. A few transfers later, I am given the officer's number, but I can't quite call him yet. I wait a few more days, and one night, well sauced and comfortably numb, I phone to thank him. That is my intention, anyway—although I am not all that sure how it goes. I can't recall what I actually say. I think I inform him that I hate suicide notes and I stopped reading them near the end of my career. My message is long and fractured.

I hang up the phone, but I don't know how to feel. I think I have done the right thing, but the right thing feels confusing and elusive to me. I sit in silence on the edge of my bed with a beer resting between my feet. I want to drink it, but my body refuses to move. After enough time, the crescendo of introspective agony sparks the motivation I require to pick the bottle up and press it against my lips. I feel the tears coming. I gulp heavily, swallowing sharply to ward off the storm in my eyes. It works; I don't cry.

I do, however, need another beer. I go to the fridge. I continue to drink bottle after bottle in hopes that the thoughts will drown themselves in a sea of silence. Instead, the thoughts just get louder.

I replay the words I had spoken on the phone over in my head and wonder if they are good enough. I am angry that I have reason to speak them in the first place. The angrier I become, the more they return—the sad scribbles of lettering etched on all the suicide notes I have read, including my mother's. *Especially* my mother's.

From the vantage point of my couch, I can see it is snowing outside. The house across the street is adorned with strands of flickering lights. On any other day at any other moment, I may have found beauty in it, but not today, not in this moment. It simply reminds me, erroneously or otherwise, that the world doesn't care. It isn't even fucking aware. The anger evolves into fire and begins to melt my insides with rage. I press the bottle to my lips once more only to be given another reason for vexation—empty. I fling my body from the couch and walk toward the kitchen to retrieve another bottle of a brooding man's medicine but find only more disappointment: I am out. No more beer. Whisky is gone, too.

I feel my hand tighten around the bottle. My fingers, wrist, and then elbow begin to dance with an agitated vibration. I stand upright, turn my body back toward the cramped quarters of my living room, take aim at an arbitrary spot on the wall, and throw the bottle as hard as I possibly can. A brilliant, glittering explosion of glass propels from wall to ceiling to floor. It cascades around my second-hand furniture and then rests along the crooked planks of my apartment. Glass is everywhere, but I don't care. I toss my boots on, grab my jacket, and slam the door angrily behind me.

I am now outside and at the mercy of the cold winter air. It is freezing. Biblically so. The wind whips at my skin without remorse or leniency. It doesn't matter. It doesn't hold a candlestick to the pain I am already in. *Bring it on, winter, you cold, cruel bastard. You got nothing.*

I find the closest bar, push my way past the door, find the nearest and emptiest section, and order more elixir of loathing. "A double, please."

I can't stop playing it in my head. And when I try, I am unable to stop myself from seeing and remembering the dead and their written words. Eventually I go home and pass out and try to sleep the next few days away.

The Mountie who found my mum, the man who took care of her, the one who read her note, the man who contacted our family, the person who helped to remove my mother from where she laid, calls me back.

"Thank you," I say.

I thank him. I thank him for looking after my mum. I thank him for making sure she got to where she needed to be. I tell him I empathize with him. I tell him I hate suicides and that I am sorry he has to see that stuff. He tells me the reason he called me back is because he has never received a message like the one I had left. He informs me he is sorry for my loss and if I am ever in town, to look him up. He tells me he would like to shake my hand. The phone call ends with me saying, "Thank you," once more. I toss the phone on my bed.

~

Months pass but my nightmares do not. I dream I am in a room. The room is void of any real detail. It is simply a room, two chairs, Mum, and me. We sit across from one another, close enough to speak quietly and comfortably.

I can't recall the entire interaction, but I know it is anything but jovial. Each word is heavy with grief. I speak first. "Hey, Mum."

"Hey, Matt." My ears ring with her familiar tone. She smiles at me, as if trying to comfort me. It doesn't work. Instead it slices like a knife, cutting deeper.

"Why, Mum? Why'd you do it?" I ask.

"Oh, Matt . . . I'm sorry . . . I am."

There is a pause and tears flood my eyes. She never reaches out to touch me. She just sits there. Waiting. Eventually I look up from the floor, and through my gloss of tears, I look at her—all her features are just how I remember them. They are not at all how she really looked toward the end. They are how I want to see her. She even has a goddamn cigarette in her hand.

I continue to ask why. Why she did what she did. Why she chose to leave this world the way she did. All I am met with is apologies. Her soprano voice and British accent attempt to make amends for the grief her actions have caused. It is futile.

As the dream progresses, so does the conversation. I ask her, "What am I supposed to do now? How am I supposed to live the rest of my life with the pain of knowing you are gone?" She does not answer.

As I feel my breath getting shorter and more panicked, I stop asking questions, and with mantra-like repetition, I recite over and over, "Mum, I miss you. I really miss you."

"I miss you, too, boy-o. I do."

In hearing the word *boy-o*, a favourite expression of my mum's, my ears snap back like a dog's acute reaction to sound, and I reach out to hug her. When she remains out of grasp, I run. I run and I run; but she keeps getting farther and farther away, always appearing just beyond my reach.

I wake up crying.

# CHAPTER 27

# Conceding

IT IS EIGHT MONTHS AFTER my mother's death, and I am sitting in Doc's office. She asks me a pointed question, a right hook of undeniable truth, "Do you feel as though you have an unhealthy relationship with alcohol?"

I want to say no, but higher thought and recent introspection override. I pause. "Yes," I answer.

We discuss the possibility of me being referred to a rehabilitation centre for treatment.

The session ends, and I skulk out of the office into the air-conditioned hallway. For the first time in my life, I am admitting that I am an alcoholic, despite never muttering the words aloud. I do not experience a profound sense of relief after this session, just the familiar self-beratement.

I board the next city bus and ride its squeaky hinges all the way to the pub. I get off and storm inside. I sit at the bar, hide my problems with a skillfully rehearsed smile and some well-timed wit, and drink the night away. Truth be told, I drink until the sun comes up. Part of me figures if I am an alcoholic, I may as well act like one.

I make the decision to put the bottle down for a few days of my own volition. My body decides to protest; I feel sick. I whisper sweet lies to myself: *I must be coming down with something.*

As a medic, I generally diagnose myself and avoid going to doctors. I don't like to feel vulnerable or susceptible to sickness. But when the symptoms refuse to go, I see a doctor.

I force my aching body to the closest walk-in clinic and wait in the holding room, surrounded by sick children with runny noses, adults complaining of vexing mystery rashes, and smokers who are confused about their shortness of breath. It is a terrible place to be, on varying levels. Eventually I am called by the charting nurse and told to head to Room 3. I wait for what seems like an eternity. I read the wall posters several dozen times. During another pass-over of said wall literature, the door swings open, revealing a doctor. We exchange pleasantries, and I tell him the reason behind my visit. As I speak, he listens, and I can't help but notice his face becoming more concerned.

"So, yeah . . . I dunno what's going on . . . I just feel off and shaky. Gross, really."

"Yeah, yeah. I hear you. Do me a favour. Hop up on the table, would you? I want to check a few things."

"Sure, no problem." I sit on top of the exam bed, and as he uses his hands and the tools of the trade to examine me, he presses for more information. I am open and honest with him and hold nothing back. I tell him about my relatively new diagnosis of PTSD and depression. I explain my sleeping problems and proclivity for alcohol. When he is sufficiently satisfied that he has conducted a thorough enough examination, he instructs me to rejoin him by the computer.

"Mr. . . . Hanna . . . Henna . . . How do you pronounce your name?"

"Uh, Heneghan, sir."

"Right, Mr. Heneghan. Mr. Heneghan, I feel no easy way to tell you this, but, my friend, you are in withdrawal. You have a drinking problem. This is why you feel poorly—your body needs that drink."

"Withdrawal? Really? Are you sure?"

"Yes. Your blood pressure is high, too high, and with all you have told me, this makes sense. You drink too much."

So now not only have I been informed by my therapist that I should enter a rehab program, but a doctor is confirming with tangible evidence that I am indeed sick from the drink.

A few days later, I return to my therapist's office for a scheduled appointment.

"Hello, Matthew. How are you feeling?"

"Yeah, good, yeah . . . good." Doc knows me well enough at this point to realize my answer is complete shit, so she waits for me to continue.

"Went to the doctor . . ."

"And?"

"Well, he thinks I am suffering from withdrawal symptoms. Gave me some pills, but I'm not gonna take 'em."

"What do you think you should do?"

"I dunno . . . I mean . . . I guess . . . I guess I gotta stop."

"Do you think you can?"

"Yeah, I mean, I stopped for like a month once. I am sure I can."

"There are places that can help you, you know." She is referring to the rehab centre we had previously discussed. I am resistant to the idea.

"Yeah, I know . . . it's just . . ."

"Just what?"

"I'm scared, Doc. I dunno what to expect."

"That's completely normal. You're entitled to feel that way; but are you going to allow that to stop you from doing what you know needs to be done?"

There is a long pause. My gaze is stuck to the floor. I want to cry, scream, and disappear all at the same time. Eventually, I lift my head and say, "I think I need to go to rehab, Doc. Let's . . . uh . . . let's set that up, please."

"We will. This is a good thing. You're doing a good thing for yourself."

"Yeah, so you keep telling me. Maybe one day I'll believe it."

"Maybe."

I leave her office, go outside, and begin walking around. The muggy air clings to my skin, saturates my clothes. I feel as though I am in a jungle, both with respect to the weather and the cluttered thoughts in my head. It's a hard thing, admitting powerlessness. I leave therapy and go straight to the bar.

That night, I drink my fucking weight in whisky and craft beers. I befriend any and all who are near me. I lie to them and tell them how great a day I am having. When that awful hour of closing time is called, I stumble out into the streets of the city. I walk home, passing alleyways laden with garbage and lost souls alike. I am even offered a beer from a homeless man I would greet from time to time. I say, "Sure."

It is two weeks before I go to rehab, and I sit outside beneath the glittered canvas of night and drink with a man who has more cans than teeth. I drink beside an itinerant man. This is an ironic situation for someone who was once entrusted with saving these people.

I never make it to my bed that night. I wake up on the floor beside the fridge. My head is heavy with regret and reality. I pull myself into a seated position and rest my back against the cold metal door of the fridge.

While doing this, amidst the fog and swirling thoughts, a voice from within speaks up. *Do you think you have a problem?* I allow the weight of my head to fall back against the fridge, colliding with a gentle thud of defeat: *Yes. Yes, I have a problem. I'm an alcoholic.*

# CHAPTER 28

# Rehab

MY BAG IS PACKED, AND I am ready to go. Well, *ready* being a somewhat relative term. I don't know that anyone is really ever ready to go to rehab. Regardless, my bag is zipped up, and I am beyond the point of no return.

Anxiety crawls through my veins. I am about to relinquish control of myself for no less than six weeks. I am supposed to believe that those around me will care for me and have my best interests at heart. As a man with trust issues, this is a less-than-pleasing yet unavoidable prospect.

I stagger over to my couch and sink into it. I know what I am doing is the right thing, but that's the thing about being right—sometimes you wish you weren't.

With some time to kill before my inevitable departure from home, I pick up my phone and dial my brother.

"Hello," he answers.

"Hey, Jonny. What's up, man?" I ask.

"Not much. What's up with you is the real question. How are *you* doing?"

"Ah, I'm fine." I'm not, of course. I force inconsequential topics of discussion to distract from the reality of my phone call, but as any good older brother does, he calls me on it.

"So, this is the big day."

"Yeah, I guess it is."

"Well, six weeks and you'll be a new man."

"Nah. Honestly, bro, when I get out, I plan to drop my stuff off and go out for a beer."

"Well, little brother, I just don't think that's what's gonna happen."

"No?"

"Look, you do whatever you gotta do. But you're going there for a reason. Try not to predict the future. Just roll with it."

And just like that, my bluff is called. I fold. He is right; I am going there for a reason. I have lost control of myself. I am in a free fall headed toward nothing good. Truth be told, I'm not too sure how much longer I would have on this earth if I didn't pack that bag.

I finish the call with my brother, put the phone down, and flop down lazily, my elbows resting on my knees. I am in distant thought when my eyes catch sight of my notebook. I had made a packing list. I decide to take one last look over the list to ensure I have packed everything I need for my stay.

I pick up the soft-cover notebook and open it to the page where I hastily scrawled my list of requirements. Little tick marks landed beside the items that had been inventoried and packed. At the very bottom of the list is an item that has not yet been checked. It simply reads: *Hope, don't forget to pack hope.*

My weary eyes linger for a moment on this last line. *Can I do this? Am I really an alcoholic? Am I really able to get sober? What if I fail?* All the usual suspects of self-doubt make their appearance known. I close the book without placing a checkmark beside it. Instead, I scroll through some old messages on my phone. I even look at decade-old discourses with my mother. Feeling a sufficient amount of self-loathing, I decide to message my friend Heather.

Heather and I have never met in real life. I met her online through a mutual friend who shared my blog with her. Heather works in the publishing world and started following my posts and took an interest in my writing. She asked me to submit a creative essay for an upcoming mental health anthology called *Brainstorm Revolution*. I did, and to my surprise, my story was accepted. Well, sort of.

"So, Matt," Heather began over the phone. "I like your essay. However, uh, well, I think it needs a little tweaking to fit the mission of the book."

"Okay." I was shocked my writing was even being considered.

She continued. "It's a little bit . . . uh . . . heavy." I could tell she was searching for words to soften the blow. "It's . . . uh . . . maybe a bit . . . dark. Bottom line, it focuses too much on the trauma and doesn't give the reader hope."

*Yep, that sounds about right*, I thought. *What's wrong with that? That is my life in a nutshell.*

She had put a mirror up to my writing, reflecting my perceived reality back at me, making me realize I saw my story as hopeless. Dutifully, I re-wrote the piece to at least hint at the possibility of hope, and it was accepted into the book. It felt a little more like fiction than a nonfiction piece, but I obliged and was very excited my words would be in print. It was a bright spot in my otherwise sorrowful life.

Heather is suspended somewhere between my mother's generation and my own. She is kind and nurturing, and we became fast friends. There is a natural maternal nature that emanates within her. It's palpable, even over text.

> Matt: Hey, Heather.
> Heather: Hey, how are you feeling?
> Matt: Nervous . . .
> Heather: I would think that is normal to feel. Are you all packed?

I take a quick scan around me and shoot a glance over to my bag. I feel as though I am, but just to make sure I pick up my notebook and take another look. With phone in hand, I snap a picture of my packing list and send it to Heather.

> Heather: I love the last line of your list!
> Matt: Yeah? Seems like something I may need to bring with me.
> Heather: You have all of us with you as well. I am proud of you.
> Matt: Thanks, Heather. Means a lot.

We chat for a little while longer, but eventually I just want to return to my solitude and piteous contemplation. My lift will be here soon.

The cab arrives, and I turn around, looking back at my apartment—a small studio living space. I wonder what it would look like when viewed through eyes that are not bloodshot or tear stained.

On the way to the centre, the driver tries to engage in pleasantries, but I am feeling less than talkative. I answer in short one-word bursts and hope he will pick up on my desire for quiet. He does. I spend the majority of the trip lost within my pounding head and the remnants of booze that slosh along the wounded hallways of my brain.

It is a muggy August day. The cloud cover is low and the buildings whizz by, coated in a thick layer of humidity. It's almost as though the buildings are crying—I can relate.

When the cab draws to a stop outside the main doors to the facility, I thank the kind man for the ride, withdraw myself and my belongings from the car, and step outside. I hear the taxi pull away. I am here.

The first thing to greet me when I arrive at this particular rehab centre is a bridge leading me from the roadway to the entryway doors. Crossing the bridge is as symbolic as it is arduous. Each step I take feels as though my legs are turning to weighted stone. I feel heavy, and my movements reflect that.

Once inside, I am met by a bright, clean, and open hallway. It is so spacious that it echoes. To the front and just off to the right sits the main desk. I assume this is where I check in.

"Is this where I register?" I ask.

"Yes, I can help you." A smiling woman assists me with the process. There is some paperwork to fill out, and then it is off to see a team of nurses and doctors. After that, it is time for a quick tour of the place. It really isn't that large of a structure, but for the first couple days it feels like a labyrinth.

Over the next little while, I grow accustomed to my new surroundings. The clients are nice and the staff even more so. I do, however, have to request a private room for sleeping because my nightmares keep my roommates awake. This is not a fun ask, but the centre is accommodating.

As the days continue to pass and my surroundings become more familiar, I am thrown another surprise—I have mail. I haven't been expecting anything, and the list of people who know where I am is exceedingly small. As such, when my name is called to the support counsellor's desk, I am unable to hide my curiosity.

"Mr. Heneghan, you have mail, sir."

"I . . . I do?"

"Yep. Came this morning. So we have to open it here at the desk with one of us present, okay? That's just standard procedure. You all right with that?"

"Yeah . . . I mean, sure. Of course."

The staff member proceeds to open the package. It is a sizeable envelope sent to me by a good friend and fellow medic, Simon. He, like many first responders, owns a sufficient amount of sardonic humour. I am curious as the staff member opens the package. I have no idea what to expect.

The first item to make its appearance from inside the envelope is Offensive Crayons, complete with an effigy of a middle finger on the box. The second item is a colouring book boasting cartoon drawings of oddly shaped penises doing unique real-world things like riding mechanical bulls and driving sports cars. And finally, the last item to plummet out of the mailer is a tiny replica of a medieval launcher. Its ammunition? Large tooth picks. That's right, my good buddy Simon mailed me a weapon while I am in a rehab facility. It is only my third day here. The look on the staff member's face is something straight out of a comedy sketch. It takes everything I have to keep myself together.

The counsellor looks at me and says, "So . . . uh . . . this is . . . well, this is something. Um . . . we . . . we can't let you have . . . well, any of this!"

"Oh, I understand. *Completely.*"

We share a brief silent pause. In his right hand he holds a medieval catapult, and in his left, some professionally drawn, triumphantly throbbing, veiny cartoon penises. At that moment, a second support counsellor comes into view. She comments on how nice it is that I have already received mail. As she speaks, her voice decrescendos into an incredulous silence.

So, here I am, as new as new can be to the rehabilitation centre, standing before two hopelessly perplexed counsellors. I am embarrassed, sure; but a mischievous part of me revels in the hilarity of it all.

That is my only package from Simon, but it is not the last piece of mail I receive. Heather takes it upon herself to cleverly carve out a small package or note a day, each containing a little riddle. In one of the daily notes, she includes a self-addressed stamped envelope and challenges me to write a letter to her: an old-fashioned, handwritten, snail-mailed form of communication. One night after dinner I excuse myself to the benches outside at the rear of the building. I sit down and read her note and then allow my pen to hover above my notepad. When I begin to write, it is fluid and uninterrupted.

Hi Heather,

You should know this is my first handwritten letter in some time—a very long time, actually! First, let me start by exclaiming my most sincere appreciation for your packages and the effort that has gone into them. Everyone around here is quite excited when it's time to open one of the mystery gifts. I must say, it certainly has increased my popularity among the clients (I call us inmates) and staff alike. Thank you so very much!

Today is the start of week three for me. I will not lie to you and spin you a tale of how great it's been because that would be a bald-faced lie. I will, however, tell you that it has been, and continues to be, a much-needed endeavour. This is the longest I have been sober since my mother's death.

With the gift of sobriety comes the burden of clear reflection and the pain it brings. I have had nightmares every night since I have stopped drinking. They even moved me to my own private room because my tortured slumber punishes not only me, but those unfortunate enough to have been doomed to be my roommate. I have shared hours of long conversations while stricken with endless streams of tears with staff members and nurses. It has been hard. But I am still here, in it through to the end. And the support from you adds to the fire of determination to see this out.

I will not have you thinking that this has been all bad—it hasn't. I have met some truly wonderful people in here: ones who will no doubt be lifelong friends. One of the more pleasing aspects of this place *is the food! My goodness, it really surpassed my bleak expectations. I was imagining army-styled mess food.*

*I gotta say, though, waking up without the companionship of a hangover is a truly glorious thing. Living day by day without the heft of the lingering fog of intoxication is . . . intoxicating.*

*I have really been feeling the loss of my mum in here. I think, perhaps, the new-found clarity that comes with sobriety, along with the anxiety and apprehension about being in a place like this, has given birth to a new wave of grief.*

*Gonna end things here.*

*Sincerely and forever grateful,*

*Matthew*

~

DURING GROUP THERAPY, I AM tasked with writing another letter. This time it is to be addressed to my addiction. I find this both challenging and fun, allowing me to be creative. At the end of my stay, we have a small graduation ceremony, and each member of our group is expected to say a few words. I decide to read my letter:

Thirty-five years, one bridge, and forty-two days: That is how long it has taken me to be here today. And now, as I sit within this room, I write this, a letter to you:

Hello, Old Friend.

As the ink of this pen begins to bleed permanence on these sheets of paper, I begin to do something that I should have done long ago—I am saying goodbye.

I have been admittedly hesitant in my dismissal of you because for so long it has just been you and me versus the world. You have been both my closest ally and my most sinister of friends.

You were there for me on that day I had to carry Andrew's flag-draped casket after his ill-fated return from Afghanistan. You clung to my hand when it was time to bid final farewells to Boomer, Starker, Wilmot, and Greg, too. And on those days that followed, when I was crippled by grief and despair, you offered a warm embrace with the promise of respite from it all.

You celebrated with me when I graduated and became a paramedic. You joined in jovially when I made my first save. And when that awful day came, and that little boy's life was lost within my hands, you stayed right beside me. Through it all, you were there.

Hell, even when we did fight, and you left me with a pain that set itself deep into my bones, I knew that I could forgive you and that once again, you would rid me of the tremendous ache that wanders the halls of my wounded mind.

On all of those days when the bad things came, the iniquitous things, you crooned to me with fables of promise and peace from it all. We were the greatest of friends in the worst of ways.

My friend, you were even there for me on the day my mother left this world. You were steadfast in your nefarious loyalty to me. For those reasons alone, I must offer a reluctant thank you. But I must also remain firm and judicious with my decision to part ways from you. Why? Because your kinship was merely a masterful illusion of friendship! You were not there for me on the worst of days any more than you were for the best of them. You simply invaded them, bafflingly, cunningly.

Not once did you truly try to help me find sanctuary from pain and anguish. Instead, you chose to foster its growth so as to ensure my dependence on you.

My friend, my dear old friend, it is not I who needs you, but rather you who requires me! And as of now, my dear friend, I am a free man. I can no longer help you, nor you, me. So, may you find peace amidst the chaos and rubble that you create. Because I assure you, it will be I who finds refuge far from it.

Goodbye, old friend. I do not need you anymore.

~

REHAB IS A DIFFICULT TASK to complete. Six weeks. It is, at times, unforgiving and painful. However, there are also moments of light-hearted buoyancy. There are days when I want to just pack it in and go home, but I don't. I stay. I stay, and I become sober. I have laughs in a place I once deemed laugh-less; I shed tears in front of strangers; and I make friends I never would have otherwise.

At the end of it all, my brother is right—I did come here for a reason, and now I leave a changed man in many ways. Or at the very least, a sober one

# CHAPTER 29

# Walking Away

THE TEETH OF THE KEYS bite into the lock, and with a heavy clunk, the door unlocks. I am apprehensive. This is the first time seeing my apartment in six weeks. Rehab is finished, and I am set free and loose into the world. The word *intimidating* comes to mind.

I walk into my apartment and let the strap of my bag fall from my shoulder as I place it on the floor. I stand still and begin to absorb my surroundings. Everything is exactly as I had left it, but it all looks completely foreign to me. This is the first time I am looking at my apartment and its contents through sober eyes. This is a unique experience, one I can't quite capture in words.

My bed is made, things are tidy and well placed, and I am just standing there, horribly torn by it all. So many memories of staggered steps, drunken tumbles, and rage-filled moments. I begin to feel and remember all of it. Then, the walls start to close in. My mind plays tricks on me as I feel the perimeter of my apartment encroaching on me with force.

After a hefty gulp and some panic-stricken breaths, I decide I need some air. I turn around and go right back out the door I had just come in. I slam it tightly behind me, lock it, and bound out the main doors of my apartment building.

I seem to have somehow developed superhuman hearing. The world, and everything alive within it, is frightfully loud. Each passing gravel truck or city bus pulverizes my senses. Although my hearing has been heightened, I do not feel super at all. I withdraw myself from the main road that runs parallel to my apartment and traipse into some quieter residential neighbourhoods. Now, instead of buses and trucks, I am mocked by hordes of screaming birds and their horribly out-of-tune chorus.

Colours are brighter, sounds are louder, and the world is more alive. I suppose this is what living looks like when you are no longer submerged under an estuary of booze. Not sure if I am liking it, I decide to go somewhere else. Somewhere familiar. A home away from home, if you will.

I walk with purpose along the sidewalk. I ignore any and all passersby and head steadfastly toward what I hope to be my sanctuary—the pub.

That's right, less than a complete hour outside of rehab and I am off to the pub. I don't feel bad about it, either. In fact, I am in a hurry to get there. When I cross at the intersection, I know I am mere feet away. I can feel my heart pounding against my sternum like a battering ram.

I skip up the two steps of the main entryway, place my hand around the handle, and pull back on the door. The pub. I have returned.

"Matty! Holy shit, you're back."

"Hey. Milo, how are you, brother? Yeah, I am back. A beer, if you'd be so kind?"

A slight pause, then, "A beer . . . ? Okay, coming right up."

Milo knows I had been to rehab; I had told him before I left. I suspect this is the reason for his slight hesitation.

I sit down in my usual spot and watch as a beer is planted on the counter before me. We engage in a cordial exchange, and I allow my fingers to wiggle like worms, inching toward a forbidden apple. Eventually, my worm-fingers are close enough to feel the cool eminence of the bottle. I throw a sideways glance, still in mid-conversation, and place the tips of my fingers to the curvaceous glass frame. I feel an instant piercing bite of cold, and chilled beads of condensation touch the folds of my skin.

When Milo walks away to help another customer, my gaze rests on the glistening bottle and takes inventory of my hand placement. A thought flashes through the corridors of my conflicted mind; it tells me to drink. It lies and says that the world will be quiet again. It whispers that I will have peace from the nightmares that had returned vengefully with my newly acquired sobriety. And for a microsecond, I almost fall for it. But then I begin to think. I mean, *truly* think. I see the faces of those I attended rehab with. I see images of me, stumbling home from the bar, looking pathetic and loathsome. I hear a voice come to life from inside my mind and it asks, *What the hell are you doing?*

I am about to undo six weeks of hard work and recovery. For what? A temporary respite from my troubles? In that moment of clarity, I am not sure who is sweating more: me or the bottle.

"Matty, you good?" Milo asks.

"Yeah . . . Hey, Milo, I . . . I gotta go, brother. Let me just settle up with you?"

Milo looks at my hand, then the bottle, the *full* bottle, and then up toward me. "Matty, this one is on me, pal. No worries."

I don't protest as I normally would. Instead, I thank him with a simple nod of my head, hop down from the barstool, and walk back out into the loud, cruel world.

It is along my directionless voyage that I take note of something: I can still hear all that I did before, but it is no longer cacophonous; it is brilliant. The birds sing harmoniously. The orchestra of the city sounds like home. Like a place where I can live and be okay. I have just walked away from a demon. Left him there like a bad date, unpaid cheque and all.

These are the first steps of self-care I take after being in rehab. From infant to toddler to recovering man all within the span of one hour, forty-five minutes, and several hundred yards of walked ground.

For the first time, I feel that maybe, just maybe, this is all possible. Maybe I really am going to be okay. But one thing is certain: No matter how it all turns out, no matter which way it all goes, I know I'll be sober through it all. I just walked away. No longer directionless. No longer stumbling or staggering: walking. Walking toward recovery.

# CHAPTER 30

# The Witch and the Bear

THE SUN SNEAKS THROUGH A pillow of thick, blanketing clouds that rest over the city. A new day is born. A dull grey hue begins to seep in through the slits of my blinds. I lie in bed while an introspective congress takes session: The bill being put forth is to legislate that I get my ass out of bed. The opposition is in favour of blankets and seclusion. Both parties lobby their arguments to the cerebral minister, and eventually the bill is passed and I am forced to sit up. I have a therapy session today, so I can't stay in bed.

I grow more aware of my surroundings and hear the hiss of tires from passing cars along the roadway outside my apartment window. The noise brings a weather report with it: It is raining, or at the very least, had been.

As I stand I notice my aching muscles and listen to their protests as my joints click and pop. *So this is what they mean by "don't get old,"* I think. With a quick and steady pull of the beaded cord, I withdraw my blinds from the window and allow the matted glow of the day to seep its way into my apartment. It is indeed raining.

Passing motorists continue to slice their way through the dampened streets as they navigate the roadways toward whatever destination awaits them. Even with the windows closed tight, I can feel the invasion of the autumn chill push its way in from the outside. *My kind of day.*

The initial pain of waking and moving soon gives way to a saturation of contentment with what I am seeing. I decide to ready myself for the day. I have therapy and some errands to run, so I plan on a quick shower and a stop at the local coffee shop for a pastry of some kind with a nice black tea to wash it down.

As I am about to move away from the window, something catches my eye. I take a second look. I am captivated by an object that is surreal yet welcome. It reminds me of my mum. It is coming up to the first Halloween without her, and the reality is hitting me hard. I have always loved this time of year, the time leading up to Halloween. Although there are a number of reasons why I adore this holiday, the overall reason is my mother, my mum—Joan.

Cancer, time spent in hospitals, her depression, and her vengeance had robbed me of a lot of time with my mum while growing up. However, around this time of year, she seemed to be her happiest self. She was rarely assigned to her bed by debilitating bouts of depression. She seemed more engaged and willing to be my mum, and I loved it.

No matter what, though, no matter how many years in a row it may have been, she always dressed up as the same thing for Halloween—she wore the complete regalia befitting a witch. She would release an unrivalled cackle that could rattle the clouds and arch the backs of cats near and far. Green face paint, a protruding mole, a pointed cap, and flowing cloak while carrying an old wooden broom, my mother was a witch—the most lovable witch you would ever meet!

As my first Halloween without my mother approaches, I am thinking about her more and more. And about the witch she so loved to be during this time. I rack my brain with ways to honour her this season. So far, all I have come up with is buying two sets of candy this year—one bowl of general mishmash, and another bowl with whole bars of chocolatey goodness. That bowl, the good bowl, I am going to reserve for only the children dressed up as witches.

So as I look out the window and see that the municipality has decorated the light pole directly outside my apartment with a straw witch, complete with a green face, a mole, and a pointed cap, I am taken aback. The witch is even wearing an outfit in my mother's favourite colour—purple. What a sight to see. What a sight for sore eyes and a pained heart. Although I chalk most things in life up to coincidences, I can't help a feeling of closeness to my mum flood over me.

I grab my coat, lock the door, and head out with a sense that, in some ways, my mum is still with me.

~

LATER THAT DAY, I AM in my therapy session. Working with Doc, as challenging as it can be, has many advantages. She is a smart woman. She has seen enough people like me (and worse) to know what to do in many situations. I no longer use booze to mitigate nightmares, and I am looking for strategies to ground myself when I come out of these terrifying and realistic dreams.

"Have you ever considered creating a nightmare basket?" she asks.

"What is that?" I have no idea what she is talking about.

"A basket of things to help ground you after a nightmare. You keep it in close proximity to your bed and fill it with familiar textiles, tools, and items you will recognize that will give you comfort after a nightmare."

This seems like a really peculiar idea; but then again, I felt that way about rehab, and it turned out she and my brother were right about that. I decide to trust her on this one.

On my way home, I buy a basket and think about what I want to fill it with. I decide to top it with items of meaning: scented waxes; a Saje sniffer—a tool of pleasing scent designed to ground me to the present; some healing rocks; a copy of *Brainstorm Revolution*, the book my creative essay is published in; and finally, a teddy bear. But not just any teddy bear. Oh, no. An exact replica of Ted from the movie *Ted*. I find some comedic acknowledgement in knowing I am a grown man who finds solace from a teddy bear.

As odd as it may be for an adult to sleep with a nightmare basket that rests beneath the glow of a nightlight, I'll take that over a man killing himself slowly in an erroneous effort to find elusive quietude in a bottle.

# CHAPTER 31

# Message in a Bottle

I WAKE UP FROM AN ungodly nightmare. It is my first Remembrance Day since leaving rehab, and I am at war. My first battle is to confront this day sober. I haven't been sober on Remembrance Day for over a decade.

I don't go to the cenotaph during the ceremony. I can't. I want to; I really do. But this morning, when I leave my house and begin walking through the chilled air, my body refuses to continue to the memorial site when there are people there. My eyes stay low, and my weighted mind forces my head to slump toward the damp, leaf-stained earth. Inflated emotion suffocates me from within. I take a sharp left and veer toward the lakefront. I walk until I can go no farther. I am by the water.

I listen to the ebb and flow of the lake and use the sounds of the crashing waves as a metronome to normalize my breathing. Once I have calmed down a little, I open my eyes and gaze across the lake bed all the way to the hazy expanse of the horizon. I think of the boys: Starker, Wilmot, Boomer, even Greg. And in doing that, I think of my mum, too. So many dead and gone. It is overwhelming, so I fabricate a story: I think about all of them being together in the same place, somewhere safe, warm, and calm. I think of how kind Greg would be toward my mum. I think of how she would enjoy embarrassing me by telling the lads stories of my youth. I even smile slightly at this fable of mine.

At the very rear of my tongue, a sinister craving creeps its way through my mouth: booze. A cold beer and a shot of whisky would dull the ache. On my way home, I force myself to stop at a coffee shop for a tea. It is beside my favourite bar, but I avoid going in.

I make it home. Remarkably, I am still sober. I want a drink more than anything at this moment. I decide to fire up the computer. I have recently started a podcast, selfishly, really. It is a form of therapy, a way to talk away the monsters. I begin recording:

Hello, everyone. This is not a scheduled podcast for me. There is no show-styled intro. It is literally Matthew, me, getting the mic to kind of give you an idea of what is going on with me today. For the first time since rehab, I really want to drink. I'd like to sit here and quench my painful thirst, but I'm not going to do that.

The reasoning behind why I'm not going to do that is I am thinking about tomorrow. That is ironic because in rehab, and most twelve-step programs, they religiously use the incantation "one day at a time." It is a great saying that has a lot of validity to it because we can't control the future. We can't control what happens tomorrow or the next day or the day after that. All we can control is ourselves moment by moment.

I know if I concede, if I were to give in to the pain that I am feeling right now and I were to reach for the bottle, and if I were to have a drink or twelve or fifteen—or however many it would take for me to not feel what I am feeling right now, I would wake up tomorrow, no doubt, hung over, in a lot of physical pain. My skin would feel heavy, my bones would ache and lament, and the pain in my soul—those scars of memory, would still be there.

In addition, I am thinking about how far I've come in these past several months, and I don't want to undo all that hard work. Now when I go to therapy, when I walk into my therapist's office and we have a conversation with one another and she gives me her feedback or she tells me things in relation to my post-traumatic stress and she is giving me treatment modalities and ideas of how thing are going to progress, I am engaged. I am not focused on being hung over. I am not worried about holding back puke in her office. I don't need to worry about those things. I am fine, so I can actually participate actively in therapy.

If I fall back and I try to get rid of the pain I am in right now with alcohol, the torment that is flowing through me, if I were to go back and use alcohol to get rid of that, I am just going to fall back into ways of old, and ways of old have led nowhere good.

I mean, I am a criminal because of drinking. You know, I have shown historically that I cannot be just a one-beer guy. I know, you know, those fleeting thoughts in my head: "Just go have one, it will take the edge off." Well one's not going to be enough. I know that. So I'm not going to go have one.

In fact, I was out for a walk because of Remembrance Day. I went by the cenotaph after the ceremony was over to say hi to the boys and thank them for the freedoms that I have today. It's Remembrance Day, and boy, that is what I am doing. I am remembering fucking everything, and it's really painful. I have no choice but to feel it. And that's the other thing about sobriety; it's okay to feel things, as painful as they may be. I am utilizing different outlets now—like this podcast where I come on and talk for a while or my blog that I still use.

I continue to ramble, trying more to convince myself than the listener that I do not need to drink. And it works. The need to drink is less powerful. I continue:

I know that alcohol is only going to act as fertilizer for my pain. I had a fire burning inside me; fire being my pain. I was pouring fuel on that fire; fuel being alcohol. Today I am not going to fuel that fire. I am just not. Fuck that fire!

Today is not an okay day. I am not okay and that is okay. But I am sober, and that's better than okay . . .

After the podcast is over, I feel lighter, better. I make a list of all the reasons why I should not drink. Then, a new tradition is born. I used to go to the bar every Remembrance Day and buy drinks for those whom I have lost. The glasses would sit in front of me, untouched and unclaimed for the duration of the night, a poignant symbol of their absence. This year I want to honour them in a new way. I want to do something worthy of their existence.

I write a story about my friends. I write about who they were and who they were to me. I speak of their sacrifice and unwavering bravery. I write of heartache, laughter, and loss. And when I am done, I print the story. I roll the paper into a scroll, place it into a bottle, and seal it tightly.

I go back to the lake, and with sadness, love, and gratitude, I throw the bottle out into the embrace of the bouncing blue waters. I feel that in a best-case scenario, someone comes across this message in a bottle and they read it. In doing so, the boys live for just a little longer before the sun goes down.

On the eleventh hour of the eleventh day of the eleventh month, I survive.

# CHAPTER 32

# Dirty Bird

ANOTHER RESTLESS NIGHT COMES AND goes. I wake up before my alarm goes off. It is yet another day saturated with significance. With a heavy soul and burdensome thoughts, I know what I am facing.

It is December 8—Mum's birthday. Or, would have been. I roll onto my back and feel the gravity of defeat push against me as I lie in bed. I look at the ceiling, recalling the features of my mum's face. I can envision her with precise clarity. I want for all of this to have been just a bad dream, one of my nightmares gone wrong. The reality is that yes, this is indeed a nightmare, but not one created from a wounded mind. Instead it is a nightmare spawned from a cruel, unforgiving world.

I blink once, then twice. Everything in front of me remains the same; my mum really is dead.

I try to will myself from bed, but my body does not move. I try to rally motivation by reminding myself this is not the first time I have been confronted by my mother's absence on her birthday. It is, however, my first time sober.

I want to honour my mum and who she was on this day, but my depression and sadness are almost too much to bear. I have had some long conversations with Doc about this approaching day. I think I have carved out a solid plan of how to cope. Turns out plans don't mean shit when confronted by the reality of grief.

When enough time passes, I swing my legs around and force myself to sit along the side of my bed. I demand better of myself. I have talked a big game leading up to this moment. I cannot allow myself to fall short of my goals. I need to get out of bed, get showered, get dressed, and get ready. I have somewhere to be and someone to meet.

I go and stand beneath the shower's perforated chrome head and turn the handle of the faucet. Soon I am enveloped by translucent beams of water, hoping to wash despair off me. It doesn't take long for that plan to fall short. I begin to weep. I am a crying man, hiding in the mist of most people's daily routine.

When all is said and done, I am showered, dressed, and standing outside, waiting for the bus to arrive. There is a cold bite to the wind today—how appropriate.

I struggle to keep outward composure; I know the bus will be here soon, and I do not want to cry in front of strangers. This task is made even more difficult by the slew of reminders of my mum: A lady walks by wearing a purple winter coat, a coat much like the one my mum once had. Across the street at the adjacent bus shelter is a woman with short hair—just the way my mum used to wear it.

While on the way to my destination, I sit by the window on the nearly empty bus. I am looking out the window, but I am not taking in the world around me. I am thinking back to happier times. I think of times spent in the company of my mum. I think back to when I used to draw her cartoon pictures for her birthday.

One year, I even got dressed up in my Sunday best: shirt, tie, and slacks. I then snuck outside and began knocking at our front door. When my mother answered, I smiled with childish zeal and informed her that I was her birthday date.

I said, "Hey, Mum. Let's go get fried chicken."

My mother, for reasons I will never know, held a rapturous appetite for the questionable delicacy that is fast-food fried chicken. It became somewhat of a birthday staple. My mum always got chicken, and you damn well better make sure she got her slaw. My mother was ravenous for dirty bird and coleslaw.

The bus stops, and the metal wail of its brakes pierces the cold winter air. I get off and walk a few hundred feet along the snow-dusted sidewalk. I stop in front of the fast-food joint.

After my mother died, I decided I was going to carry on the tradition of procuring greasy chicken for her birthday. On the first year after her death, I ordered what I thought she might like, ate some of it, and then proceeded to obliterate myself with countless beers and old-fashioned whiskies. Let's just say that throwing up fried chicken is not a good way to remember anyone, especially my mum.

This year is different, though. I am sober. I walk inside and place my order. I stand quietly and wait as they do whatever it is they do behind those counters. They call my ticket number, and I grab the tray. I find a booth near the back of the restaurant. I have someone to meet, at least in spirit and in thought: my mum.

No one in the restaurant can see her except me. My tradition is to go get fried chicken and have a dinner date with my mum. And this year, I do it with a clear mind and untainted blood. I might cry, but I won't throw up.

I miss my mum. I miss her so very much. Not a day goes by that she does not come across my mind. I am heartbroken about the pain she was in. I feel grateful to have had her in my life for the brief time I did. I am, and will forever be, appreciative of all she has done for me. But one thing I will never understand is, *Why the fuck did she like this chicken?*

# CHAPTER 33

# Holidays

I PEER OUT MY WINDOW AND watch daylight fall toward the other side of the world. As the sky fades to black, strands of Christmas lights on top of streetlamps and business signs begin to illuminate like hand-plucked stars that have been placed on Earth just for the season. It is beautiful. I love Christmas. Well, historically, anyway.

Although staring out at the twinkling scene is somewhat peaceful, inside I am anything but. I can't remember a time when I did not have a drink at Christmas. As a kid, I was always allowed a glass of wine at dinner, and sometimes I would sneak a little extra throughout the evening, too. This year I am confronting the season as a sober orphan. I am doing my best not to dwell on that.

~

LATER IN THE DAY, I finish my session with Doc and walk toward my bus stop, but I suddenly turn and head to a nearby mall instead. I decide to look for an apartment-sized fake Christmas tree. I have not had a tree for years and make a conscious decision that this year I will baptize my apartment with its first Christmas adornment. It may be a small decision in most eyes, but for me it is monumental. I know that Mum would want me to have one.

I search and find the perfect one, a small pine number. It comes in a box small enough to carry to the bus. *Perfect*, I think and head back to the bus stop.

I get home and begin the tedious chore of unpacking this boxed holiday symbol and, piece by piece, it begins to take shape. When all is said and done, I admire the four-and-a-half-foot fold-out pine. It even has lights already attached, so all I have to do is plug it in and bask in the captivating ambiance of its Christmas glow.

I imagine this is how Charlie Brown felt when he stood before his own forever hopeless tree. I find myself involuntarily saying, "Well, Ma, what do you think? Pretty great, right?" In a surprise flash flood of thought, it starts to feel like Christmas for me.

When I think back to my work as a medic during the holidays, some difficult memories surface. I have worked as many day shifts as I have night shifts at Christmas, a notoriously busy time on the ambulance. I feel myself getting lost in the time warp of my thoughts. I shake my head slightly and pull out my Saje sniffer, making sure to ground myself to the present.

I consider calling my older brother, Jon. I had told him earlier in the week that I may do this, get a tree. I take a picture of it first and text it to him. I walk over to the coffee table by the TV and reach for my phone, but I am halted by an unexpected knock at my door. Having a proclivity for hearing thuds and wallops that are not taking place in the present, I wait to see if I will hear the sound again, tightly holding my Saje sniffer. The knock comes again—someone really is thumping at my door.

I leave the phone on the table and apprehensively go over to my door. I peer through the viewing hole and see a mailman standing, swaying in place, waiting. I twist the lock and pull open the door to greet the letter-bearer.

"Hello?"

"Oh, hey. Merry Christmas. I have a package for you. Matthew, right? Sign here."

I do. He hands me a brown padded envelope and walks away down the hall while smiling and whistling. My forehead wrinkles as I head back inside. I am not expecting anything. I look to the top corner of the envelope. It is Jon's return address.

My face stains with confusion. I consider impulsively tearing into the package, but I stop myself. Instead, I place the package on the counter and retrieve my phone. I call Jon.

"Hey, brother," Jon says. I can hear his children in the background. Their voices compete to be heard. He encourages them to go and play and then returns his attention to his end of the phone. Though I am not there, I can almost see everything that is happening.

"Hey, Jonny. Did you send me a package, brother?" I ask.

"Sure did," he confirms. "You get it?"

"Yeah, it came just now. I didn't know you were sending me anything."

"Well, it's a good surprise, then, isn't it?"

"Yeah, I'd say. Thanks, man."

"No problem. You open it yet?"

"Nah . . . want me to? Or should I wait until Christmas day?"

"That's up to you, little brother. You do what you want. I'm just happy it made it to you."

I pause for a moment, holding the package in my hand. As I gaze upon it, the lights of my brand-new Christmas tree begin singing to me. I look up and over at the tree . . . more specifically, at the bottom of it. There is a lot of empty space under there. It has been well over five years since I have had a Christmas gift under my own tree. I decide I would like to have a gift waiting for me on Christmas morning. With my brother still on the phone, I walk over and place the package beneath the resting branches of the tree.

"I'm gonna wait, bro. This will be the first gift that I have had to open on Christmas morning since . . . meh . . . it's been too long."

"Well, there ya go . . . got yourself something to do come Christmas . . . hope you like it."

"I love it!"

"You opened it?"

"No . . . but, Jon . . . I love it . . ."

My brother is not much of an outwardly emotional guy, so his silence confirms that I am welcome. We say our cordial goodbyes and make plans to play some online games later and chat over the headsets. I walk over to the couch and plop my weary body down. I am grateful for the gift, but I am having trouble fighting the dissonance that comes from knowing this medic's body and aching mind will have no Christmas shift to report for. The core of why I became a medic was because I wanted to make a difference in people's lives. *But now what? What can I do now to make a difference?* This question haunts me for the better part of an hour. I think I secretly held out hope that when I became sober, I would also be free of PTSD and could one day go back to work on the ambulance. *A fool's fantasy.*

It suddenly occurs to me that I am still thinking *like* medics as opposed to *about* medics. What I mean is, I am still contemplating what it's like to be at work during these days and nights instead of thinking about those who are actually at work. This is when it dawns on me: *I know what I can do to make a difference. A small one, but one nonetheless.*

I pick my phone back up and begin to search for and dial the numbers to the local ambulance, fire, and police divisions in my area. I speak to whomever answers the phone. I say these words: "Hey . . . Look, I know this is likely going to be an unorthodox call, but I just wanted to reach out and say thank you. Thank you for working during the holidays. Thank you for sacrificing your time with your family so we may enjoy time with ours. What you folks do is truly invaluable.

"I just want to let you know that there are people out there that love, respect, and care for what you do. And I hope that no matter what happens on shift tonight and over the next few days, you find time for a hot lunch, warm coffee, and some time to relax. You deserve it . . . you all do."

This is another tradition I decide to enact as a sober man. I think my mum would approve of it, too. She is the one who always taught me to say thank you.

# CHAPTER 34

# My Name Is Matthew

I POST A LINK TO my latest blog on Twitter, and I get a retweet from Theo Fleury. *One of my hockey idols liked one of my posts? Wow!* I liked Fleury as a hockey player, but I fell in love with his courage after he stopped playing. He was so open and raw when speaking about the abuse he had suffered at the hands of those he was supposed to be able to trust. It was awe inspiring. Still is.

I am in Doc's office today, usual appointment. I want to tell her something, but I can't get the words out. Each time they scurry to the tip of my tongue, they are met by the ivory guards of my clenched teeth. At one point, I think I might be able to say something to her, but I don't. The session ends, and I just pause awkwardly at the door for a moment too long and say, "Thanks for your time."

I stand outside in the company of a cold winter's wind for a little longer than I should before making my way home. I am distracted and despondent. I see a man and his son walking on the street. The boy looks to be about nine, the same age I was when my father was taken away.

Without the numbing effects of alcohol, my buried layers of supressed memory are resurfacing. I don't talk about these memories very often, mostly because part of me is still so ashamed. I can count on one hand the number of people to whom I have confessed them. These recollections are hidden in a small, carved-out section of my being that is held hostage by fear and perception. I worry what the world will think. I am petrified of what people might say, the looks I might get, and, to be honest, part of me just wishes it wasn't real.

There is a pilot light of anger hidden deep inside me. It never goes out. The flame doesn't flicker or falter. All the other clutter tries to crowd around it, blocking it from view. But the burn is always there beneath the thinnest layer of my inked skin. There hums a static of agitation and pain. As a kid I was never allowed to talk about it. It was relegated to a section of banished topics.

I take transit home and fire up the computer. If I can't tell Doc what I want to say, maybe I can write it. I start an email:

I have spoken about my father, provided skeletal details of him and who or what he was. I often refer to him as a bad man. And to me, that's true. I learned only one thing from him in my life—I learned what kind of man NOT to be. I was also gifted a permanent reminder of the things he did—a man who hit kids with belt buckles, fists, and feet. His legacy is a craggy, Braille-like scar along my back.

I have been somewhat open about the physical abuse I sustained at his hands. What I have been a little more shamefaced about is the other abuse, the other things he did, the things he did at night, the things he did to me. I can still hear his voice, even now. I was too young to really be able to recall a lot of things, a blessing maybe; but some things are painfully present within the compartments of memory.

As an adult, I was finally granted access to the court documents pertaining to my father and the abuse he had put us through. I learned that I have three sisters I have never met. I learned of other kids he had done this to. I read of the physical abuse toward me and at what age it started—at the age of two. Terrible twos, indeed.

I am writing this because it has been bubbling beneath the surface for a few days now. The ignition of further thought came after seeing Theo's "like" on my post. I envy his courage and dedication to recovery. It takes a kind of bravery I don't think I have. Theo speaks so openly, and I am afraid to write this. I am also afraid to go to sleep—I have been dreaming of an ominous figure as of late, a figure that feels horribly familiar. I still cry sometimes.

I am writing this because I am ashamed. I am. But I don't want to be anymore. I want to help that kid, the kid inside me. The one whose only light is from an angry flame. I. Want. To. Talk. But the words are like knives. Each laceration feels like a wound of embarrassment. Even as a medic I don't know how to heal that.

All I know is that it is a poison. I feel like a coward for keeping it in, and I feel like a fool for speaking of it at all. Logic brain says I shouldn't be ashamed or judgmental toward myself, but currently I am sitting with a frightened kid around a pilot light, and neither one of us knows how to turn it off.

My name is Matthew, and I was molested.

I hesitate, then hit SEND on the screen. I email a copy to Doc and another to Heather, who is in Ottawa on business.

Then the worry and incessant contemplation sets in. I don't hear much back from Heather other than a few words saying she is sorry for what had happened to me. I sit in my apartment in fear of judgment. Finally, I can't take it anymore and I message her:

**ME: Hey. Can I ask you a question and you will give me an honest answer?**
**HEATHER: Sure. Of course!**
**ME: Do you think I'm a freak?**
**HEATHER: What?! No? Why?**
**ME: Because of what I told you.**
**HEATHER: Matthew, you were only a kid. I don't think any differently of you. IT'S NOT YOUR FAULT. I am truly sorry this happened to you. You are a survivor and have absolutely nothing to be ashamed about.**

I try to absorb her assurance of "It's not your fault," but it is hard. I know that one day, when I let this secret free, its power will lessen. I am ready to do that; I am ready to heal.

# CHAPTER 35

# Suiting Up

MY BLOG GARNERS SOME ATTENTION, and I have been asked to speak on Valentine's Day at a theatre event called Unconventional Love Stories. The fellow presenters are also contributors to the book *Brainstorm Revolution*. The event will consist of a collection of storytellers sharing their journeys on stage in a quaint theatre in Barrie, Ontario, a city about an hour's drive from where I live. The story I will share is about my mother and Thanksgiving. I am grateful to tell a happy story about my mum to others. It is a couple of weeks away, but already I am both excited and nervous.

I need something to wear for this event, so I make my way to a local men's shop.

"What size do you need, sir?" The store clerk's eyes widen, awaiting my response.

"Uh, extra large, please," I say.

"Sure thing." He sifts through the rack, using his hands to push from one jacket to the next, his tongue peeking out from between his pursed lips.

"Ah! Here we are—one extra large, as requested." He hands me the jacket and asks if that's all I require.

"Yes," I answer, and we walk to the front of the store together. He cashes me out and I leave. I stand outside, waiting for my taxi, watching as a rolling plume of smoky-grey clouds cover what little blue was left in the sky. Just before the cab arrives, a splash or two of rain land on top of my forehead. On the way back to my place, the rain intensifies and so do my thoughts.

I have been alive and on this planet for thirty-six years. In that time, I have worn a total of three suit jackets (one of which does not really count). The first was my graduation suit (this one is kind of a given, I suppose). It was a gifted double-breasted pin-stripe handed to me in celebration of completing high school. The second—well, that was a little more rigorously earned—the forest green of my military-issued dress coat. I wore that jacket, and only that jacket, for six years. I wore it to weddings, Christmases, graduations, and yes, many funerals. Then, when it was time to hang that jacket up, I donned another jacket of service—the jacket of a paramedic. The weight of a city and its people was embroidered within crests that hung heavy on my shoulders. And when it was time to hang that one up, too, I was lost. Naked. Directionless and lonely.

Today is the first time I have spent my own money to buy my very own jacket. The jacket rests beside me in the car on the way home. It is tucked safely away within the zippered garment bag.

"Are you going to a wedding?" The taxi driver queries.

"Me? Oh, no. No, sir. No weddings for me. I have an event to go to later this week. Figured I should look the part, you know?"

"Ah, handsome?"

"Something like that, yeah. Can't do much about my face, but I managed to wrangle a nice jacket, so we should be good," I say through a forced smile.

I arrive home and manage to get inside before suffering any consequences of the now falling sheets of rain. I place my jacket atop my bed and let it rest in the bag. I wander over to the kettle and plop it on the burner, then wait.

Out of the corner of my eye, the bag and its contents beckon. I resist at first as I initially feel no need to re-examine what I already know to be inside. But without obvious reason, I find myself standing over the bag, unzipping it. I reach inside and pull out the jacket. I think about the invitation extended to me to share my story, a small piece of it, anyway. I imagine the venue, the people filing in, taking their seats, and listening as I share something I have written. Something else floods over me, something distant but recognizable. It takes me a moment, but then I identify it: a sense of purpose.

I decide not to hang my purchase up in the closet quite yet. Something is holding me back. Instead I suspend the hanger from the closet doorknob, where the jacket will remain in full view.

~

IT'S FOUR IN THE MORNING, and I am awake. I am awake before the automated beep of my alarm goes off. My aching mind and its often-treacherous thoughts push me toward awakening. Pain, anguish, and traumas once lived percolate within the coffee maker of my memory before dripping into the cup of consciousness.

It is a Wednesday morning, the eve before the theatre presentation in Barrie. I should be excited, but my brain doesn't always do what I think it should. I roll onto my back and toss glances into my mind's imagery. I see my mum's face and then her note. Though I have not read it since that day, each scribbled line is permanently nailed to the inside of my mind.

In the ungodly quiet of this early morning, I read from memory each of my mother's last words. I do not do this willingly; it is a symptom of a broken heart belonging to a dented man. I am also a boy who has lost his mum. My father, a child molester. My mother, gone. Killed by her own mind. My family? Scattered within the debris of childhood trauma and the recent loss. I suppose it makes sense I was awake after all: A troubled mind is not often a restful one.

I am due to be in Barrie for 5:00 p.m. tomorrow, Valentine's Day. As such, I decide to head up a day early so I can rest and not have to worry about travelling the day of.

I pull myself out of bed and grab my bags and place them by the front door. I spend the next little while getting ready before calling an Uber to head up toward Barrie. My friend Danny arrives at my apartment. He is coming with me for moral support and company. I am grateful; he is a good guy that way.

As we head out the door to catch our ride, I pick up my bags and, of course, my new jacket.

After we arrive at our hotel, I am somewhat excited because I know Barrie and want to visit some of my old haunts. I spent a decent portion of time as a young man here. When I was in the army, my base was just west of the city, so weekends were typically spent there, hopping from bar to bar.

After we unpack and settle in, I take Danny to McReilly's, a pub and eatery on the main drag of town. It is made up of old wooden beams and creaky floor boards that speak beneath the unsteady gait of its patrons. I'll never forget the night that Morris had a few too many black and tans and puked into the stein before discreetly placing it underneath a nearby table and then ordering some deep-fried cheese sticks—and another black and tan.

The place is exactly as I remembered it, despite the decade or so that has passed since I was last here. I walk inside and lead

Danny to my usual spot. A feeling of nostalgia is sparked when the table we sit at begins to wobble beneath the weight of our resting elbows. When I say nothing has changed, I suppose that's not entirely true. The menu has been given an overhaul and the walls are covered by a new coat of paint. Other than that, though, it is the same ol' McReilly's.

Danny and I sit and have a bite to eat. Danny appears to enjoy the retelling of some of my more mischievous army days, and I enjoy sitting in a room of memories that don't haunt me at night.

After a quick walk about the town and a dip in the hotel pool, it is time to begin settling for the night. The TV is on, but it acts merely as background noise for me. I am reading in preparation for my story the next day. I practise saying it aloud a couple of times and ask Danny for feedback. He says it is good and seems genuine in his critique. Feeling the weight of a long day, I finally begin settling in to sleep. Well, I try, anyway. It is horror free, but it is a restless night, nonetheless.

# CHAPTER 36

# The Chairs Are Purple

DANNY AND I LUMBER FROM our respective beds and begin to pack up to meet with my friend Heather. She is one of the organizers of the event. She arrives with an accompanying aura of eagerness and drive, no doubt completing checklists in her head.

She takes us to the theatre to meet with the staff and check out the venue.

"Hey, can you help carry some of these boxes in?" she asks as she pops the trunk.

"Sure," we oblige.

A worker from the theatre holds the door open, and I manoeuvre past her while carrying one of the boxes. I enter a dimly lit entryway at the back of the building and make a sharp left to walk down the stairs. I manage one or two steps before the nefarious nature of PTSD takes hold, engulfing my mind with jostling images, tastes, and smells from my memory.

*Clunk, clunk, clunk!* My heavy steps slap the wood of the stairs as I descend farther and farther into the bowels of the theatre. The descent is not just physical: My mind free-falls into the past.

The act of entering a doorway, making a sudden and sharp right, then traipsing downward ignites thoughts of the boy, the fourteen-year-old I had once responded to as a medic. On the day I found him, it was at the bottom of a set of old wooden stairs, much like the ones I am now on.

As I near the base of the stairs, I am confronted by an archway to my left—just like at the call. I fully anticipate making a required left turn and then seeing a dead boy swinging from a rope by his neck. I round the corner—no boy. No musty basement. No frantic sibling trying to cut a brother down while pleading for me to help. I am now fully in this story because internally I am somewhere completely different from where I now find myself.

The gift of sobriety and a clear mind is that I know what is happening before ever involuntarily reacting to it. At least not fully. I am able to convince myself I am not in the basement of a dead boy's house. I am able to acclimate to the here and now. My nose, however, is not so fortunate. A sudden and sharp introduction of odorous urine begins hijacking my sense of smell.

Heather is speaking to me, but I am not sure what she is saying or why she is saying it. The next clear sequence of events that I can remember is Heather asking, "Are you all right?"

I attempt to explain my odd demeanour. I begin to choke on both my words and the taste of urine. I break. My eyes fail me and let one tear go, then another.

I cry, horribly so.

Heather gives me the time I need. She comes to check on me at some point when I have collected enough of myself to be somewhat coherent. She is kind and understanding with me. However, I am not so generous with myself. I feel bad. I feel as though I have done something wrong. She reassures me otherwise, but it remains no less frustrating for me. I mean, here I am, in the theatre of the place where I am going to give a presentation of my own story about my mother to complete strangers, and I can't even remain present for it. I feel vexed and dejected.

Fortunately, something serendipitous takes place.

I want to recall fond memories of my mother, and I want to share those memories with the world and keep her alive for a little while longer. This is why this presentation is so important to me. I want to do well. I want to tell people just how incredible a woman she could be. I suck up the remainder of self-loathing and shove it to the rear of my priorities and follow Heather up a different set of stairs that lead into the main part of the theatre.

We walk into a dark room bordered by dark curtains that hang beautifully from ceiling to floor. The overhead lighting is subtle and pleasing to the eyes. It is exciting to see where this event will take place. As the theatre assistant talks details and logistics with Heather, my eyes scan the room. I gape in marvel at it all. This is a real theatre. *A legit place for the thespian. Or, in this case, the talking wounded.*

And that's when it happens, when my eyes cease all movement and rest solely on the chairs. *The chairs. The chairs are purple.* My story is about my mum, my pain is of my mum's absence, and my memory is of her life, a life she lived with an adoration for the colour purple. My mother loved it. Purple everything.

I am taken aback for a moment. I have just come from the hell of downstairs and am now standing in a room where my mother is on every chair around me. It feels as though she is saying, "It's okay, Matty-wat. It's okay, you're okay. Mum's right here. Mum's right here."

The topper for all of this is that I have a chair reserved just for her, my mum. It is complete with a "reserved" placard and everything. My mum is right here in this room, all over the place.

The evening rolls around and all the presenters congregate, chatting and eating in the green room. I know many of them already as I have met them previously at a book signing. They are also writers who have contributed to the anthology *Brainstorm Revolution*. I am both nervous and excited.

Right before the show is to start we head up the stairs, the main stairs in the front, not the set that had triggered my flashback. We take our seats at the sides of the theatre and the presentation begins. I am the third speaker. Before I know it, I find myself walking over to the podium, story in hand. I clear my throat and start to talk:

The table was a sprawling tapestry of culinary delectation. My helpless nose was seduced by the meandering aromas that filled the living space of our home. It was Thanksgiving, and my mother had spent the working hours of a day confined to her laboratory, the kitchen.

Throughout the day, I was filled with a youthful sense of entitlement as, much to her dismay, I snuck in and out of my mother's area of comestible dominance. I couldn't help myself. Those sweet smells enticed my nostrils to the point of ravenous desire. No matter where I was within my home, I could smell it. Taste it. Picture it and then begin to crave it all the more.

My mother had started her preparation early that weekend morning. I woke to the soft, redolent, and ethereal conjoining aromas tapping against my nose.

Its effect was that of a gleeful spring from my covers as I took flight from my mattress.

My mother's cooking was second to none. Now, I know we all say that about our mothers, and I am sure it is true. Your mother was likely an amazing cook . . . but not like my mum. No way.

Happy to not only have the company of the succulent rising aromas greet me that morning, I was also able to see a trundling sea of low-hanging rain clouds resting overtop our little town. The perfect day to be thankful. And thankful I was. As well as excited.

Thanksgiving was always a good time in our family. There was typically very little in the way of drama or tension. And a plethora of gluttony to be had. My mother would go all out.

I said she had started early that morning, but I am pretty sure she had planned out what she was going to make and how she was going to make it weeks in advance— and it always paid off!

I've always loved this time of year. I loved it then and I love it now. The time of year when the leaves don a regalia of yellow, orange, and cardinal red. It's the time of year when that slight chill in the air sneaks past your skin and tickles your bones. There is always hockey on the TV and a game going on outside on some quiet little side street. Staccatos of wrist shots and slap shots are taken until perfection is reached. Blisters on the hands don't matter—there's a game to win.

Looking back, I grow more fond of that time in my life. And that is because of my mother's presence on those days of thanks. In the present, I am still fond of this season and this holiday—but I am aware of a certain sadness that now hangs around with that little chill in the air . . .

My mother's not here . . . not any more . . .

But she was back then. My mother would spend hours on her aching feet, sifting through pluming clouds of flour as she punched and kneaded dough into perfect consistency. She would tear whole loaves of bread apart with mathematical precision and toss them into a bowl where magic would happen and stuffing would be made! Ah, my mother's stuffing . . . there is no substitute.

And in the background, immersed within a sea of its own juices and savory decadence, tucked away within the warm embrace of the oven, the turkey—*my God, the turkey*—seasoned with a hidden recipe of flavours and love. It took hours to cook (much to my dismay) until it was a golden brown, featherless, and headless torso of delight. It was perfect. Something so beautiful that you didn't want to eat it—until you tasted it. Then you would savagely inhale its tenderness. And inhale I would.

I would forgo any semblance of proper dining etiquette and unrestrainedly devour every scrap, every morsel of food that had been placed on my plate. I was allowed a glass of wine on occasions such as these. I would often pause, raise my glass to my lips, and feel the diminutive bubbles leap and explode with brilliance onto the tip of my nose. Turkey and white bubbly—what a mix.

I have not had a meal prepared by my mother in over a decade, a regret that I will carry with me for the remainder of my days in this life. It is not that she has been dead for decades—quite the opposite, actually— she has only been gone for a matter of months. Months that feel like weeks. And weeks that feel like days. And days that are more akin to hours. And hours to seconds. Life got in the way is all. Seemingly so . . . and now, it's too late. She's gone.

I am sad that my mother is no longer here. I am angry that it was suicide that took her . . .

I hear a woman in the front row gasp. News of my mother's death deflates her lungs the same as it had mine on that cold Tuesday morning in November. I try to continue, but each time I open my mouth, nothing comes out. I am choking. My throat is being strangled by a remorseless grasp of grief.

I open my mouth once more in demand of continuance, but all that falls from it is a bewailed sound of loss and pain. It punishes the microphone in front of me. My grief now washes across the watchful crowd, piercing loudly through the speakers of the theatre.

I take a step back from the mic and put my hand up to my eyes as if shielding myself. I know I have to finish the story. I *need* to.

I quickly wipe the tears from my eyes, and in doing so, I accidentally dislodge a contact lens. How fitting—I am blind once again, just as I had been as a child when I wore the red and blue cape my mother had lovingly made for me. I had to win. The kryptonite of grief would not stop me from allowing my mother to live through this story.

All of this occurs in a matter of seconds, but in this moment, it feels like hours. I gain composure and continue, reciting the rest of my prose from memory:

I am bewildered by the reality of it all. But I am also grateful. I am blessed to have had such moments in the past where my mother was alive, well, and happy.

Now, this Thanksgiving, as I walk with heavy steps over to my fridge and remove the single-serving pot pie and plop it into the oven, I can hear her laugh. Something I have struggled to recall over these painful few months. I am grateful I can hear it. What a poignant, euphonious sound it is. Yes, I am grateful for it all.

I am delighted that I possess memories such as the one I shared with you. Many people do not. I am thankful to have been loved and to have loved such a woman as my mum. I am overjoyed that I am still loved by those around me. I have amazing people in my life. People who care for me with endless amounts of energy. I am fortunate to be alive and well.

> I may be lonely without my dear mum and her talents in the kitchen, but I am for certain not alone—and I could not be more grateful for that.

As I finish, I look up through a misty gaze and a misplaced contact lens floating around somewhere in my eye. I see my mum's reserved seating sign and her purple chair. *Victory!* The entire room, as if on queue, stands, clapping.

That night I am supported by those around me. I am hugged and given words of kindness. Complete strangers come up and thank me for my story about my mum. An elderly man walks up to me and tells me he could envision everything I was saying, and although he had lost his mother over thirty years prior, he could remember her as clear as anything while I told my story. Compliments don't come much higher than that.

The end of the evening rolls around. As I am packing to leave, a friend and fellow author, Maud, puts her hand on my shoulder and says to me, "Everyone needs a blankie."

I am unsure what she means at first. But then I remember a social media post I had written recently about being afraid to sleep and equating my fear to that of a child without his blankie. Maud had made me a blanket. I now have *my* blankie, thanks to her.

~

Danny and I take an Uber home, and I am quiet during the hour-long ride. I am dropped off at my apartment first. I unlock the door, walk in, and immediately get ready for bed. As I hang up my suit jacket beside my other two, I wonder what its significance will become. It dawns on me that it was precisely two years ago to the day that I landed in Doc's office. I am also exactly six months sober. What a difference two years can make. Although I have no idea what this jacket will grow to represent, I acknowledge that I now have hope that the future at least holds *something*. And like the jacket itself, this realization is new and exciting. As I hang it in the closet for the first time, I take comfort in knowing that it won't be the last time.

I crawl into bed and feel the fleece embrace of a blanket made with love, stitched with generosity, and given in sincerity. I close my eyes, and the first thing to varnish the backs of my eyelids is an expansive sea of purple: *The chairs, the chairs are purple . . .*

I fall asleep. No nightmares. No bad smells. No screaming wounded. Nothing but contentment and rest. That's a pretty great love story for Valentine's Day.

*Mum, thanks.*

# ACKNOWLEDGEMENTS

To FIT ONTO ONE PAGE or in one place the number of people whom I would like to thank is impossible. For this reason, and this reason alone, I am choosing to highlight only a few—and please note that it is not because of hierarchy of importance. Please know, to all those who have helped me along the way and to those who have supported me in this troubled life, I am forever grateful.

I would like to take this opportunity to thank with utmost sincerity Dr. Carol Heusser, Ph.D., C. Psych. Without your guidance, professionalism, and dedication to care, I would not have been able to see past the darkness of my own clouded mind through to the other side toward hope. I am a changed man who is forever appreciative of your service and skill.

Doc, you're reading these words today because you kept me alive. This is why I am able to write them—thank you.

Further, I would be remiss should I not mention how grateful I am to all those who have spent long hours editing, reading, then re-reading, and critiquing this story of mine. A special shout-out goes to V.N. Doran and Patricia MacDonald for their feedback and expert editing skills. I would not have been able to tell my story the way I wanted to without these people; this is their accomplishment, too.

# ABOUT THE AUTHOR

BORN IN THE UNITED KINGDOM, Matthew Heneghan immigrated to Canada at a young age. He grew up in rural British Columbia where he learned the value of friendship and lending a helping hand. Matthew went on to eventually join the Canadian Armed Forces as a medic. His career was cut short by the beginnings of post-traumatic stress disorder. He went on to serve as a civilian paramedic until he could no longer remain healthy in his job.

Matthew has faced a variety of challenges in his life, including his decision to get clean and sober. Throughout his many adversities, Matthew has discovered the value of hope. His main goal in life is to help others, maybe no longer with the original plan of being a medic, but by encouraging people who see themselves in his words.

Matthew is an avid speaker and podcaster. He also writes a blog. You can connect with Matthew on most social media platforms.

@amedicsmind

amedicsmind.com

*ISBN 978-1-894813-95-2*

Brainstorm Revolution: true mental health stories of
love, personal evolution, and cultural revolution.

CPSIA information can be obtained
at www.ICGtesting.com
Printed in the USA
LVHW031352141019
634125LV00007B/2771/P

9 781894 813976